THE HONORABLE SELF

Also coauthored by Brooks and Church:

Subtle Suicide: Our Silent Epidemic of Ambivalence About Living
How Psychology Applies to Everyday Life
The Dysfunctional Relationships of Givers and Takers
Using Psychology to Cope with Everyday Stress

Also by Church:

Avoiders: How They Become and Remain Depressed

The Authors' Website: *www.subtlesuicide.com*
The Authors' Blog: https://psychologyandstressblog.com/

THE HONORABLE SELF

Manage Stress with Humility
and Empathy

Charles Brooks / Michael Church

To order additional copies of this book, contact:
Xlibris
844-714-8691
www.Xlibris.com
Orders@Xlibris.com
819110

CONTENTS

Preface vii

Chapter 1   Honor and Coping 1
Chapter 2   Acceptance 19
Chapter 3   Accountability 37
Chapter 4   Humility 53
Chapter 5   Empathy..66
Chapter 6   Planning..96
Chapter 7   Relaxation Exercises................................ 135
Chapter 8   A Word About Depression 143

Postscript.. 157

PREFACE

This is a book about psychology and coping with stress. But it's also a book about character—traits like integrity, morality, and values.

We recently published a basic self-help book, *Using Psychology to Cope with Everyday Stress*. We offered what we consider to be important psychological principles of coping with life's challenges:

There are only two things you can directly control: *your* thoughts and *your* actions.

You must accept and face your emotions for what they are—a part of you.

Inappropriate actions, not your emotions, are the coping problem.

Effective coping requires performing optimistic, realistic actions, not merely thinking positive thoughts.

Personal happiness emerges within those actions that bring you intrinsic satisfaction.

Seeking personal pity parties are avoidance actions that disrupt effective coping.

You have no right to have the corners of your world padded for you.

You are not here to live up to others' expectations.

Actions must be guided by a social conscience, values, and ethical standards.

Recent events—the coronavirus pandemic, protests and riots in some cities, and questionable morality, truthfulness, and character in political leaders—got us to thinking that the last item on that list of principles above—"Actions must be guided by a social conscience, values, and ethical standards"—did not receive the attention it deserves in our earlier book.

In fact, we began to think that without these character traits—"honor," if you will—effective coping simply cannot succeed. Originally, we liked to think of coping with stress as involving a three-part process:

(1) *Acceptance.* You must resist the temptation to engage in denial about situations that bring you uncomfortable emotions. You must accept reality and your emotional reactions to it.

(2) *Accountability.* You must take responsibility for all your actions, not just your mistakes. But you must also hold others accountable for their actions.

(3) *Plan of Action.* You must develop one. Coping means action. Effective coping means actions based on confidence and patience—actions that are rational, organized, realistic, and logical.

OK, that's all well and good. But for a complete coping strategy, we need to add three more components to the process:

(4) *Values.* You must base your life on a set of moral guides that provide you with a sense of personal direction.

(5) *Humility.* You need this. Coping can't be "all about me."

(6) *Empathy.* Finally, and perhaps the most important, effective coping requires understanding yourself that emerges from understanding others. That doesn't mean you must feel sorry for them. It means that you can resolve conflicts better, and feel more independent and empowered, when you act with the needs of others in mind.

In this brief book, we expand on *Using Psychology to Cope with Everyday Stress* and try to bring those last three components—values, humility, and empathy—into clearer focus as crucial components to the coping process. Taken together, we have chosen to combine all six components into what we call an honorable self. We believe that the development of understanding who you are, and how you fit in the challenging adventure of living your life, is greatly enhanced when you keep before you the importance of maintaining your honor—your integrity, ethics, decency, morality, and conscience—and finding your honorable self.

Throughout this book, we give hypothetical examples of people wrestling with issues relevant to our discussion. We use these examples solely to expand and illuminate an understanding of the coping principles being discussed. The situations described are completely fabricated, and the people in the examples are fictitious.

CHAPTER 1

HONOR AND COPING

Kevin is fifty-six, a former construction worker who is widowed with two sons who are married and live two thousand miles away. Kevin is on disability because of a work accident from several years ago. Physically, he can handle most normal everyday chores and activities, as long as he avoids heavy lifting. In other words, there are a lot of things Kevin can do. However, he spends most of his days at home feeling sorry for himself—watching TV and dwelling on how stressed and depressed he is. His self-esteem, self-confidence, and initiative are in the toilet.

He was once a burly, outgoing guy loaded with motivation, a can-do attitude, and a willingness to confidently take on any job at his work site. One of his coworkers described Kevin as someone who always "had a fire in his belly that when work needs to get done, he's the one to do it."

Then came his accident and his wife's death from cancer. His behavior switched from "out of my way, I can handle this" to "I'm not much good anymore." His mind lost its harmony—when beliefs and self-concept are consistent with one's actions—and sent out SOS signals in the form of anxiety and depression.

Emotional disruptions are your mind telling you,
"Things are out of balance!"

One day came a call from Jim, a friend: "Kevin! I need help. I have to deliver for Meals on Wheels today, but I pulled my back, something terrible. I can drive OK, but getting in and out of the car is agony. Would you come with me and take the meals up to the door?"

Kevin was glad to get out of the house and said he would help. Turns out, he had some unexpected and remarkable experiences when he delivered the meals. When he knocked, one woman yelled out, "It's open! Just bring it in. I can't get to the door very good!"

She was in the kitchen, and Kevin put the meal in the fridge for her. He started for the front door, but she grabbed his arm and said, "Pray with me, please."

Kevin returned to the car and told Jim, "I stood there holding her hand, while she thanked God for me being there to help her. Prayed for me! I mean, no one ever thanked God for me!"

Jim said, "Yeah, Gladys is a doll. Really makes it all worth it, doesn't it?"

Kevin just muttered softly, almost in amazement, "She prayed for me."

And on it went as Kevin went to the front door at each stop. No one else prayed for him, but nearly every one of them said, "God bless you" or "You're a saint, sir. Thank you," as he left.

One old guy was on his computer, which surprised Kevin—"I didn't know old people knew how to use a computer." He printed out a page with inspirational sayings on it about the importance of taking care of your neighbor. He handed it to Kevin. "This is for you. Bless you for living these words. Thank you so much." Kevin was speechless.

He got in the car and said, "I swear to God, Jim, I thought I was going to cry."

Jim just smiled and nodded.

Kevin got home that day, looked around the house, and realized that he suddenly felt better than he had since his accident and his wife's death. As Kevin told Jim later, "I picked up the phone and called the Office of Aging. Said I wanted to volunteer to deliver meals. The lady said great and added that they also needed drivers to taxi old folks around to their doctor appointments, take them shopping . . . wherever they needed to go. I said, 'I'm your guy, ma'am. Just tell me what needs doing, and I'll get it done.'"

Ah, the rejuvenation of Kevin. The confident, can-do guy of old was back. What a beautiful thing to see. But what happened to bring on this awakening? It's pretty obvious, isn't it? Kevin's mental harmony was restored as he stopped focusing on his emotions and how miserable he was and started to focus on helping others. He took himself and his pity parade out of the equation and allowed his mind to find the old can-do Kevin by focusing on others. He found his honorable self through service to others. Some might say he was born again!

He "found his honorable self." What on earth does that mean? To answer that question, please understand that effective coping is a journey. It means you are alive. It is not a goal you put on your calendar to reach by that date. Coping is something that emerges from your actions, your perspectives, your expectations, and surprisingly, your character—in short, your honor.

You're wondering, "Personal honor is something that can help me cope with stress?" You don't usually associate honor with coping, do you? When was the last time you heard someone say, "I'm having such a hard time coping with the stress in my life. I guess I need to be more honorable"? Probably never, right?

If a friend asked you for advice about how to deal better with stressful events, probably the last thing that would occur to you would be to say something like, "Well, to start, you need to find your honorable self." If you did say that, you would, no doubt, see one of those blank, deer-in-the-headlight expressions on your friend's face, an expression saying, "Huh?"

Honor is not a characteristic we generally associate with handling stress. When you think of stress, you generally think of things like how to relax, how to become more confident and assertive, or how to organize your life better. But honor? No, that's for people who are fighting, engaged in warfare, sports competition, not coping with stress.

Maybe it's time to make personal honor a part of your coping plan.

Honor is a trait based on values, and your values are crucial if you want to cope with stress effectively. Many folks just live for today. They don't plan, and they don't take risks because they are afraid of venturing out of their comfort zone. This "safety strategy" guarantees—at least they believe it guarantees—that they don't have to experience things like disappointment, failure, rejection, responsibility, and loss. But at what cost? Are they really human or just existing? What are they so afraid of and avoiding? What are they not accepting? What are they denying? We will get to these and other questions, but for now, let's take a brief look at what we mean by honor.

<>   <>   <>

HONOR AS A PART OF COPING

What is honor anyway? The Cadet Honor Code at the United States Military Academy in West Point, New York, reads simply, *"A cadet will not lie, cheat, steal, or tolerate those who do."*

The code at the Air Force Academy says, *"We will not lie, steal or cheat, nor tolerate among us anyone who does. Furthermore, I resolve to do my duty and to live honorably (so help me God)."*

The honor concept at the United States Naval Academy in Annapolis, Maryland, goes into a little more detail, but the same idea as the other academies is there: *"Midshipmen are persons of integrity: They tell the truth and ensure that the truth is known. They do not lie. They embrace fairness in all actions. They ensure that work submitted as their own is their own, and that assistance received from any source is authorized and properly documented. They do not cheat. They respect the property of others and ensure that others are able to benefit from the use of their own property. They do not steal."*

Honor—it's easy to think of in military terms, and that is why the notion plays such a large role in the mission of our military academies.

But honor should also be an integral part of living because it will help you cope with everyday challenges. How so? Personal honor will help you critically evaluate information that comes to you each day. Honor will also help you make a plan of action that will allow you to live your life interacting with yourself and with others in a way that helps you avoid selfish actions. Honor will allow you to look in the mirror with satisfaction at the end of each day and say, "I did OK today."

"Wow!" You think, "That sounds great. But how do I make those things happen?" It's simple, really. Just remember that effective coping rests on a tripod: *acceptance* of what you do, *accountability* for the consequences of what you do, and *planning* to improve the quality of what you do. Living a life of honor will help you build that tripod as you critically examine your daily life.

To conduct a critical examination of yourself, here are some basic questions—ones that deal with honor—you might ask yourself on a regular basis:

"Do I try to deceive and manipulate others for my own selfish ends?"

"Do I care when I see others being deceived?"

"Are my actions based on selfish entitlement to gain unfair advantage of others?"

"Am I able to understand how others feel when they are troubled?"

"When I consider my actions toward others, do I ask myself how I would feel if I were at the receiving end of those actions?"

Keep in mind that you also have a right to challenge others so you can vaccinate yourself against excessive dependency on them. Thus, you should also ask "honor questions" about actions others direct at you:

"Do they try to deceive and manipulate me for their betterment?"

"Do they seem to care about my feelings?"

"Are their actions based on selfish entitlement to gain unfair advantage over me?"

"These things they ask of me—how would they feel if I asked the same of them?"

Asking such questions can engage you in the critical thinking required for resisting excessive dependence on others and facilitating the development of what we call your honorable self.

But notice one important thing about those questions: In addition to the acceptance/accountability/planning triad, they bring in two more dimensions to your self-evaluation—*humility* and *empathy*.

"Do I try to deceive and manipulate others for my own selfish ends?" If you do, you have no humility. "Am I able to understand how others feel when they are troubled?" If you are not able, you have no empathy.

Of course, effective coping requires you to feel confident and empowered to be capable of independent action. Without humility and empathy, however, you will drift into narcissism and feel that you are above it all, someone special. Humility will teach you that you are not the prime ingredient in the recipe.

Empathy will complement that teaching and show you that the path to true self-understanding—the way to an honorable self—is through understanding and serving others. When it comes to effective coping, traits like honor, integrity, and character are always "in"; narcissism is always "out." When you see the latter, whether in yourself or in another, reject it like you would any other poison.

<>   <>   <>

FOCUS ON INFORMATION, NOT EMOTIONS

Hank's a nice guy, well-liked by his colleagues at work. For the most part, he likes his job, although there are parts of it he hates. He hates to travel. He hates being in a room full of strangers. He hates public speaking. Hank likes being in his comfort zone—working alone at his desk designing human resource policies to improve production, employee morale, and establishing ways to measure company goals. After work, Hank loves being with his wife and two sons, ten and twelve. They're active in community activities like Little League, youth soccer, and fundraising in the neighborhood. Hank's a good guy.

Hank's boss calls him in one day and says, "There's this big workshop day after tomorrow on improving employee relations. It's over in Middleton [fifty miles away], and I want you to represent us. There'll be a lot of reps from other companies, a breakfast social hour, big social function for lunch, presentations, and small workshops. All in one day! You'll need to be there at eight, and you'll be home by seven easy."

Hank cringes silently. He hates this sort of thing and gets very anxious about it. "I'll do nothing but worry about this for the next two days," he thinks. "All those strangers. Having to talk at those workshops. Why didn't he send Will?"

A couple of days later, at 7:45 a.m., Hank finds himself pulling into the parking lot of the hotel hosting the workshop. He thinks, "At least I got here on time. Now stay calm, Hank. You'll be fine."

"Stay calm," "I'll be fine"—those comments are called denial. Hank knows he's going to be nervous—in fact, he already is—but he's trying to convince himself things might be different this time.

Denial—the polar opposite of acceptance. When you go down that road, you're doomed, like a student taking a test without studying for it. When confronted with a situation that has always made you anxious in the past, never tell yourself, "I won't be anxious this time." You *will* be anxious, but now you will be totally unprepared to deal with it.

Back to Hank. The preliminary coffee/Danish social hour has started. He walks in the room, and fear strikes his heart as he looks around and realizes he doesn't know anyone. On top of that, everyone in the room is talking with someone, laughing with them, and having a good time with their friends. At least that's how Hank perceives it: "I'm the outcast here, the lone ranger, the one guy here who knows no one. God, I hate this."

And then the self-criticism begins: "I'm going to look and sound like a total idiot. They're all going to wonder, 'Who's that poor soul without a friend in the world?' I'll never make it through this thing. If this gets back to the boss, I'm screwed! I'll just grab a coffee, hang out at the food table, and wait for the program to begin. Maybe staying in the restroom until then would be better."

Can you identify Hank's focus? He's obsessing about how he feels, his anxiety. He's focusing directly on the emotion he's feeling and desperately wondering what he can do to *get rid of the emotion*; first, *denial*, which leaves him totally unprepared to deal with his anxiety, and now *avoidance*, his only recourse after denial kicks in. Hank is dreadfully anxious about being around all those strangers, and all he can think of is how to escape so he won't be so anxious.

> *Focusing on unwanted emotions leads to denial and*
> *avoidance, self-defeating actions that add to anxiety.*

Hank focuses on criticizing himself by assuming he will be the laughing stock of the room. He creates a pessimistic, self-fulfilling prediction that he will be overcome by anxiety and helplessness.

He is focused on himself, his emotion, hardly a sign of humility, and begins thinking irrationally. He assumes he is not living up to the expectations of others and seeks an avoidance strategy so he doesn't have to confront and accept his fear. This is a recipe for a coping disaster.

> *Hank makes himself the primary ingredient and forms a*
> *personal pity parade.*

How can Hank turn this agonizing situation into a challenge and not a threat? First of all, note that his task has been complicated because he began with denial: "Stay calm." Had he accepted the inevitability of his anxiety—"I'm going to walk in there and feel really anxious. But that's OK. It's who I am. What I need is a plan to work through the anxiety"—he could have prepared himself in advance, instead of working on the fly, so to speak.

So what can Hank do in this anxiety-laden situation? Various techniques are often suggested, such as deep breathing and thought-distracting techniques. We will examine some of them in detail in chapter 7, but for now, let's consider a couple of methods that involve more psychological strategies.

Hank could *challenge the irrationality of his thinking* while standing in the room. "Let's face it. No one is paying the least bit of attention to me and my anxiety, and if they are, so what? Am I going to die? They might even know someone at my company if I bother to tell them where

I work. Come on, Hank, get with it. Just head for the food and coffee and ask some folks where they work and let things go from there. Ask if they know the presenter, have ever heard her before, or ever been to an event like this. Simple stuff, small talk. These people are not here to judge me."

"These people are not here to judge me." Now there's a thought. Hank could suddenly realize that he's not the center of the room; the others are not there with him in mind. A humble insight, isn't it, and one that's pretty realistic. Such humility can have a calming effect.

Realistic and humble self-talk, not self-critical, can diminish anxiety.

Rational self-talk like that can indeed be helpful. There's also a technique that may work for Hank, one people seldom hear about. First of all, Hank can take note that his discomfort is caused by specific characteristics of the situation. In this case, it is a *crowd* of *strangers*, and when he entered the room, he automatically defaulted to concentrating on what he saw as a threatening situation. What if, instead of focusing on *crowd* and *strangers*, Hank distracted himself by focusing on using additional information provided by the people in the room to speculate about them?

For instance, he could survey the room and think, "I'll use their manner of dress—color of clothing and accessories like lapel pins and jewelry—to guess what office they work in at their company. Could be human resources, payroll, budgeting, distribution, sales . . . places like that. Then I'll strike up a conversation and ask them."

It's simple to do, and it will help. Why? Because focusing on analyzing information will help Hank concentrate on a task, a problem to solve, and get him away from focusing on his anxiety. The anxiety focus is emotion-based and sets Hank up as a self-perceived martyr to be pitied. Focusing on information is task-based and allows Hank to take himself out of the equation and solve a problem.

So Hank picks a guy standing over at the food table. He's alone, not talking to anyone, and looks like he's trying to decide on what kind donut to pick.

Hank decides that with his flamboyant tie, he's got to be in sales. He walks over next to the guy, chooses a doughnut, and says, "Glazed looks good. How's it going? Are you with Amalgam Products? You look familiar."

"Amalgam? No, sorry, I'm with Fairfield."

"Fairfield. I've heard it's a great company with a quality sales department. You in sales?"

The game is on for Hank! What happened to that anxiety? Hank is beginning to find his honorable self and not let his emotions rule him.

ACHIEVING MENTAL HARMONY

The human mind loves harmony and consistency, and when you feel stress and anxiety, it's often a signal that things in your mind are out of balance. For instance, George is a single-parent father of a fifteen-year-old girl who has been arrested for shoplifting. George feels he is a tolerant and understanding dad, a reasonable disciplinarian, and a good source of parental guidance. And yet his daughter is in trouble with the law! His self-perception and his daughter's behavior are not harmonious. As a result, George is under a lot of stress.

George decides his daughter needs counseling and medication, so he sets up an appointment with a psychiatrist. He also forbids her to hang out with a certain group of peers, and he monitors her social media activities. Unfortunately, nothing seems to work. His daughter remains hostile, uncooperative, agitated, and often downright nasty toward him. George struggles to cope as the imbalances in his mind continue to bring him considerable anxiety.

A major part of George's problem, of course, is that he has trouble examining his role in his daughter's behavior. He doesn't see how his actions contribute to her problems, many of which are a normal part of navigating the psychological and biological minefield that is adolescence. His approach to the problem is self-absorbed, keeping himself as the dominant element in the equation. He can't find the empathy to see things from his daughter's perspective.

The best prognosis—unfortunately, we do not know the outcome of George's case—for George is to make sure his daughter's counseling sessions include him so he can begin to see how his lack of empathy is contributing to the strains in their relationship. If George does not move in this direction and work hard at establishing more empathetic lines of communication with his daughter, the prognosis for their conflict is not encouraging.

We would also hope that the psychiatrist does not automatically turn to medications for the daughter. As we said, many aspects of her issues—and certainly, his issues as well—are part of the standard "storm of adolescence" and might not require psychiatric meds.

We have seen many college students who seek advice and counseling in college because of similar issues with parents that we see in George's daughter, although without the arrest record, which can complicate things if a pattern develops. One thing for certain, however, when the student has been on psychiatric medication for a number of years during adolescence, much of the learning and discovery about oneself in relation to others is missing. The result is a lack of mental harmony because the self-concept is so poorly developed.

<> <> <>

DOTH YOU PROTEST TOO MUCH?

Karla's best friend, Tara, texted, "K, stop by on your way home so I can show you my new outfit!" When Karla visited later, Tara was wearing the new clothes and said, "Don't you just love it?"

Truth be told, Karla thought Tara looked hideous. She thought, "Omigod, they don't even match. Plus, the shoulders droop on the blouse, and the slacks make her look twenty pounds heavier. Crap. What do I say?"

"Is this a knockout outfit or what? On sale too, so I got a great buy."

Karla decided she didn't want to deflate Tara's balloon. "She's on such a high over this stuff, I can't bear to tell her what I think. I'll bring her down gently later," Karla thought to herself.

"It's nice, Tar," Karla said weakly. "I'm really glad you found something you like and at such a price. You always were good at finding the bargains!"

Karla lied, right? Yes, but some might call her lukewarm praise diplomatic, tactful. She didn't want to ruin her friend's happy moment by being brutally honest, so she fudged a bit with a "white lie." No harm, no foul, right?

We all do it now and then, a little deception out of respect for someone's feelings. They treated you to a movie you hated, bought you dinner at a restaurant you hate, or gave you a present you can't stand. In each case, you bit the bullet, thanked them, and said how enjoyable it all was. Nothing to lose sleep over *as long as eventually you find a way to correct the lie.*

Correct the lie. Karla did that by waiting a couple of days and saying to Tara, "I've been thinking about that new outfit you got. It's nice, and you're really good about picking clothes, but it just doesn't bring out your natural good looks. Something's not right . . . maybe the color. Hey, let's go shopping tomorrow where you got it and see if we can get something even better!" Karla corrected the lie, complimented Tara, and involved her in improving things. That's coping with honor!

Note that originally, Karla acted and spoke the opposite of how she really felt. When done in moderation, and to spare hurting someone's feelings, we call it diplomacy, being considerate. But what if this behavior is chronic, habitual, your customary way of dealing with others to make them think you are something you are not? In this case, we have what psychologists call the ego defense of *reaction formation.*

For instance, what if Karla didn't feel comfortable correcting her lie? What if she was worried that doing so would make Tara mad and jeopardize their friendship? What if she didn't have the self-confidence and personal empowerment to suggest to Tara that the outfit really wasn't the best choice?

In these cases, she sure wouldn't suggest that they shop for something better. But then Karla would have a problem: Her lack of honor in not correcting her lie would cause her to feel guilty about lying to Tara, even if it was well intended. She might be aware of the guilt or not, but either way, she has created a stressful situation for herself. What to do?

She could engage in *reaction formation*, which would involve praising Tara regularly—excessively—about her good taste and also praising her to others. Friends may even begin to notice: "Karla, why are you constantly reminding us that Tara should be a fashion designer because she has this incredible taste in clothes? I mean, OK, we believe you. Just let it go."

Shakespeare said it in *Hamlet,* when he had Queen Gertrude comment on the excessive insincerity of a character in a play, "The lady doth protest too much." Karla's friend is basically saying, "You know, Karla, the way you praise Tara all the time makes me wonder if you really mean it." And that's what *reaction formation* means: behaving outwardly the opposite of how you feel inside in order to hide—from yourself and others—those inner feelings that cause you anxiety.

Exhibiting chronically extreme behavior signals insecurities.

Gene, thirty-eight, has a high-stress job with a stock market group. The workers exist solely to make money for their clients by choosing how to invest their clients' money in the market. Gene has a so-so record with the company—a few successes, more failures—but you would never know it.

Whether at work or in public, Gene prances and struts around like the head rooster in the farmyard. He boasts to anyone who will listen about his prowess, and he's always eager to criticize his colleagues. He wears the best clothes, drives a super expensive car, and lives in an apartment beyond his means.

Gene's arrogant behavior is extreme, well beyond what he can logically justify. Yes, he had his share of successes at work but also many failures. A psychologist would look at his excessive bragging, with all the material trimmings, as designed to hide and avoid facing some internal conflict.

A knowledge of Gene's childhood would uncover his core insecurity: Gene was raised by an authoritarian, demanding father who could never be pleased. No matter what Gene did, Dad found a way to criticize it. He hits a homerun in Little League, but Dad reminds him he struck out twice; he got a B+ in chemistry, but Dad wonders why not an A. Get the picture? Dad always managed to belittle Gene's successes, which kept his son's self-esteem in the toilet.

Gene's adult behavior shows *reaction formation*: Inside, he is insecure and afraid of failure. His extreme overt displays of confidence are smoke screens—ego defenses—designed to hide those internal fears. His displays of competence and independence are intense and chronic, and they betray in him a desperate attempt to hide his anxieties and weaknesses from others, especially from himself and from Dad.

When used as a defense mechanism, *reaction formation* is like all ego defenses—a form of denial. Gene looks in the mirror and sees an immaculately-dressed man smoking a king-sized cigar. That vision allows him to deny what he knows is really inside him: a frightened, insecure wimp desperate to please Dad, fearing the slightest hint of failure will lead to rejection and abandonment. The outwardly successful-appearing Gene is really a frightened child.

In our earlier example, Karla was not showing *reaction formation* when she told Tara she liked the new outfit. She was simply showing some empathy, and she corrected the deception later. We noted, however, that if she failed to make that correction, she becomes Gene, deceiving herself by taking on extreme actions to hide insecurities.

Keep an eye on your actions, and ask yourself if you have become Gene. The original Karla dynamic—correcting her lie with humility and empathy—is an example of coping with a stressful situation with honor. The Gene dynamic—behaving outwardly to hide internal insecurities—is one of denial, avoidance, and instability, a dishonorable pattern that will end up causing a lot more stress.

<> <> <>

HISTORY SHOWS WE'RE NOT UNIQUE

People often try to cope with their insecurities by blaming others for their problems. For instance, would you be surprised to hear someone complain, "You know, it's a wonder any of us are sane. I mean, look at all the stressors around us: Social media is filled with lies. We have regular reports on TV about horrible things going on in the world. We have huge cities that are noisy, polluted, and overcrowded. People run to the suburbs to the country to escape it all, and what happens? The suburbs become noisy, polluted, and overcrowded."

It's a great rationalization, isn't it? You're feeling stressed from all these pressures. How can anyone be expected to cope well? No wonder there's such an increase these days in mental disorders!

There's a long list of things and people in society that you can blame for your inability to cope. You've really got it bad these days, worse than any other generation, right? Wrong!

Excuses for stress problems are nothing new, so stop
making them.

In the late eighteenth and early nineteenth centuries, in both Europe and America, so-called nervous disorders were increasing dramatically, especially among women. Today these problems would be called anxiety disorders and would also come under the general rubric of coping with stress.

Practitioners of the day blamed the increase in these nervous disorders on the stressors of "modern" civilization: the railroads, which made a lot of noise and transported people around very quickly; the telegraph, which gave almost instantaneous communication and could spread bad news easily; the noisy, dirty cities that took people away from the serenity of nature; the increased proliferation of print sources like newspapers and magazines that contained disturbing news.

Sound familiar? From a stress perspective, just how different, really, is 2020 from 1900? Like you, people in 1900 had excuses and scapegoats to blame when they were having trouble coping. And amazingly enough, the agents of blame were the same as used in 2020!

"But wait," you protest, "we also have a pandemic." Sorry, the Spanish flu hit in 1918. Also, Americans had that little disturbance called WW1 to worry about around the same time.

The point here is simple: Your stressors are neither unique nor worse than anyone on the planet has ever experienced. That pity parade doesn't square with reality. So you might as well *accept* your problems as a part of life, make yourself *accountable* in facing them, and develop a *rational plan* to cope with them. Sounds pretty empowering, doesn't it?

PASSIONATE COPING

In the late eighteenth century—the time of our revolutionary founders like Adams, Hamilton, Jefferson, Madison, and Washington—describing someone as being "passionate" about an issue meant they were very emotional about it but not necessarily in a good way. Getting "passionate" when a particular topic came up meant getting "bent out of shape," being "too worked up," exploding emotionally, and having difficulty with self-control when discussing the issue. Excessive passion meant being overly emotional about an issue to the point that it clouded good judgment.

When it comes to effective coping with stress, in eighteenth-century usage, becoming passionate about an issue would be counterproductive because excessive emotional outbursts would make rational and reasoned examination of a conflict difficult. Becoming passionate would produce defensiveness, frustration, and even hatred, sending calm deliberation out the window.

What "passionate" means today, of course, is different from two hundred years ago. Today, if you are passionate about something, you are immersed in it—committed and dedicated to the issue; you love it and find it worthwhile and satisfying. Be it music, science, serving others, or childrearing, being passionate suggests a devotion to effort and always striving to improve.

Each year college admissions committees try to bring in a "well-rounded" class of students with diverse interests. The committees do not want cookie-cutter young people who all fit the same mold. Except for one thing: Passion! Admissions committees want students who are passionate about life and learning and about at least one special activity that gives their life meaning, purpose, and motivates them to achieve important goals.

When it comes to coping with stress, you must find passion about your life. This doesn't mean you love every aspect of your life and jump from one enjoyable aspect to another. No, passionate coping means you value life in general and believe it is important to be an active participant in life.

Being passionate encourages you to engage yourself in both the good and the bad aspects of living: You strive to "connect," not avoid, even when faced with challenges. You become devoted to effort, not ambivalence. You plan rather than withdraw. You seek achievement, not stagnation. Connecting, striving, planning, and achieving are effective coping strategies because they are honorable. These activities honor the self because they celebrate accountability and responsibility.

As tennis star Billie Jean King once said, "No matter how tough, no matter what kind of outside pressure, no matter how many bad breaks along the way, I must keep my sights on the final goal, to win, win, win, and with more love and passion than the world has ever witnessed in any performance."

So many people just live for the moment. Their life road is one of avoidance so they don't have to experience disappointment, failure, rejection, responsibility, loss, and other pitfalls that are a part of living. Remember, however, avoidance may be easy, but it comes at a cost. It guarantees a life of fear and anxiety. It guarantees a life of denial. It guarantees a life of dependency and uncertainty about who you are. Those who avoid and deny—are they really human or just existing?

In this book, passion means having honor to guide you in living your life. It means striving to be all you can be and feeling satisfied for having made the effort. It means being honest with yourself and with others. It means behaving in ways that create and reveal self-respect. It means discovering your essence by exercising a social conscience. It means understanding, respecting, and serving others. It means following your values, your principles, your standards, and your goals. It means living with a purpose.

CHAPTER 2

ACCEPTANCE

Like everyone else, you have stress in your life, and you want to be able to deal with it. The first step is *acceptance*. This can be a tricky concept because a lot of people confuse acceptance with giving up, being passive, and resigned to the inevitability of stressful events swirling around you. Passivity and helplessness, however, are not at all what we mean by acceptance.

Acceptance is the opposite of avoidance, which involves actions like denial, irrational thinking, and passively accepting what others tell you. Acceptance means empowering yourself, facing yourself and the reality of events around you. Sometimes those actions mean working through some pain and suffering, but that is often necessary if you are to grow and reach contentment.

<> <> <>

BEING WHO YOU ARE DOES NOT MAKE YOU WEAK

The challenge of facing who you are starts pretty early in life for most people. How many parents have heard comments like these from a young child?

"Mommy, I don't like my name. Can I change it?"

"Daddy, why am I such a scaredy cat? Why can't I be brave like you?"

"I hate my curly hair, Mommy. Can you straighten it?"

Sure, these things are standard kid's grumblings as they struggle to come to grips with who they are. But these concerns can easily extend into adulthood as we continue to compare ourselves with others.

Jessica is a nineteen-year-old college student. She's a real high achiever but goes a little overboard by expecting herself to be close to perfect. She says,

> My parents always drilled in me the importance of doing things right. Sloppy work was just not an option. OK, I can live with that, but what drives me up the wall is that I get so anxious and angry at myself when I fall short of perfection. Why am I like that? Why can't I be like my brother who shrugs it off when he blows it and just says, "No big deal. I'll do better next time." So laid-back, so cool, so in control. But me, I'm there biting my fingernails off!"

Striving for high-quality work is admirable, but if you fall short and cope with emotions using self-criticism, you're not coping well. First, you're teaching yourself to be self-critical, and you'll never be satisfied with your work, even when it's good. Second, self-criticism ignores the fact that striving for perfection is usually better than being sloppy and uncaring. Finally, self-criticism treats your emotions like your enemy, and that treatment denies who you are.

You messed up. You're frustrated, anxious, angry. How should you handle your emotions? The key to answering that question is to accept how you feel and admit it's a part of who you are. Then you should be able to think about your emotions a little differently.

If you're mad at yourself for being overly perfectionistic, pause and consider the positive aspects of this trait: First, you're less likely to make foolish mistakes. Second, you are showing others that you care about the quality of your work. Third, you are more likely to seek creative solutions to a task. Fourth, you are less likely to depend on others for completing a task. Fifth, you demonstrate how your actions are consistent with your values.

Jessica can remove her self-criticism by focusing on these points. She can also remind herself that her perfectionistic tendencies are consistent with how she was raised and taught by role models she respects. "I was always taught that I must act in ways that make me proud of the result. If I'm going to do something, do it right. That's my value, and it's the principle I live by."

> *Instead of criticizing yourself for who you are, accept*
> *who you are and examine the benefits of your traits.*
> *This analysis can increase your sense of control, personal*
> *empowerment, and autonomy.*

Suppose you're anxious and fearful about something going on in the world. Someone tells you, "Don't worry, everything's going to be fine. You're worrying over nothing." Does that comment make you feel better? It shouldn't because that advice is saying, "Just deny what's worrying you."

But suppose you listen to this advice and say to yourself, "Yeah, you're right, I shouldn't be afraid. Everything will work out. I'll just stay calm." Does that make you feel better? We hope not because once again you are being asked to deny something, in this case, the part of you that is anxious and fearful.

Don't deny how you feel! You must accept your fear as real. Also, accept the fact that you can use your fear to your advantage. Just as we showed how being a perfectionist can work to your advantage, so can being fearful and anxious work for you.

Accepting the reality of your fear as a part of who you are can have a calming effect that keeps you in a steady frame of mind. Your anxiety can also help you stay alert and focused on developing plans to attend to the fearful situation. Finally, your concern can help you stay vigilant and monitor the effectiveness of those plans as you implement them.

The result is that your plans are more likely to be successful because you are operating with a positive sense of independence and empowerment that emerge from acceptance. Remember, acceptance of who you are is a fundamental step in coping with stress. Always work from that foundation of acceptance. Denial of the reality of who you are sets in motion a destructive sequence that will be self-defeating and toxic for your coping efforts.

> *Denial of your emotions brings dishonor to your sense of self. "This is not me" leads to "I don't like myself," which leads to "I'm unworthy," which leads to feeling helpless when confronted with a challenge, which makes you vulnerable to depression.*

Once you accept yourself and find ways to make it work for you, honorable coping will be the result. It's like telling someone, "Yes, I'm too [*insert any emotion that bothers you*], but it's who I am, and I make it work to my advantage."

I DON'T CARE

I [CB] recently saw an item on Facebook describing how a celebrity felt about a social issue. The post generated hundreds of replies, with just about every comment falling into one of three categories: (1) "I agree," (2)" I disagree," (3) "I don't care how this celebrity feels."

It's that last category that caught my attention. I mean, why would people who don't care feel compelled to take the time to let the world know that they don't give a rat's backside about how the celeb felt? That doesn't make sense. If you don't care, why the need to comment?

Imagine being a counselor and having a client who was dealing with a variety of anxiety issues. During one session, the client tells you how his best friend betrayed him by sharing information with others that the client had told this friend in confidence.

While telling the story, the client's eyes begin to "well up" with tears. As he wipes his eyes, he says rather defiantly, "I don't care though. Screw him."

You might be tempted to respond, "That's interesting. You say you don't care, but I guess some part of you cares because a part of you is weeping about losing a friend."

Could we pose the same response to folks who post on Facebook, "I don't care what this celebrity thinks"? A response along the lines of "Well, that's interesting, but it looks like some part of you cares because some part of you needs to announce your apathy publicly."

Logically, if you don't care about something, shouldn't you just ignore it? How often do you observe habits in others that are different from yours? You might say you don't care about their habit, but do you make a big deal out of it or just ignore it?

Imagine having a meal with some folks, and one of them says to you, "I see that you eat all of one food on your plate before eating another. Of course, I don't really care about your eating habits. How you eat is up to you." If that happened to you, would you think that your "critic" might have some insecurities triggered by your eating style? Would you be tempted to say, "If you don't care, why do you need to bring attention to my eating habits? What's that all about?"

Here's the point: When you have a need to announce, "I don't care," for all to hear, you are including yourself in that audience. Could it be that the situation has tapped into some unresolved psychological conflict that produces anxiety, although at an unconscious level? Your mind, of course, doesn't want to face that anxiety. What better way to avoid it than to announce loudly to others and to yourself, of course, that you "don't care" about this issue. You are basically trying to convince yourself that it's OK to avoid facing the issue. After all, "I don't care."

The truth is, however, you *do* care, and you may be showing a need to deny something inside you that you would prefer not to face because you feel insecure about it. Sounds crazy, I know, but people have many ways of showing denial.

Taking time to bring attention to something but then saying,
"Of course, I really don't care," shows a misaligned disconnect,
indicating that an event has tapped into an inner conflict.

Of course, saying "I don't care" can be, and usually is, a frivolous, off-hand comment, especially when you are replying to a question like, "What do you think of that?" You look puzzled and say, "Are you serious? Apparently, you have me confused with someone who gives a damn."

If, however, you voluntarily offer the "I don't care" assertion, as in our eating example, it can be a sign of an inner insecurity that may be worth accepting and facing. Be vigilant for the "I don't care" signal; you might learn something new about yourself or others.

One final thought—when you go around being critical of others' personal choices and habits, you are not behaving honorably. You are intruding in disrespectful and discourteous ways. You are showing selfishness and condescension by implying that your ways of doings are superior. These dishonorable actions are almost guaranteed to bring stress and conflict into your life.

<>   <>   <>

WHAT DOES IT MEAN TO "MOVE ON"?

Any advice on coping with stress will eventually use some variation of the phrase "move on." For example:

> "This situation is not under your control, so it's time to move on to other things bothering you."
>
> "You've confronted the problem and done all you can do. Now the ball is in someone else's court. It's time for you to move on."
>
> "This is not a time for you to be ruminating about yesterday. What's already happened can't be undone. Time to move on and deal with the present."

The interesting thing is we all seem to assume we know what is meant by the words "move on" and that moving on is often the best course of action. This assumption, of course, begs the question "What do you think 'moving on' means?"

We asked some folks this question, and not surprisingly, the answers generally revolved around a common idea: "Moving on means putting something behind you; it means realizing that you can't do anything about something, so you should put it out of your life, out of your thoughts, and forget about it."

In most cases, in the context of coping with stress, we disagree with this interpretation of what "moving on" truly means. To illustrate, let's consider Dorothy, a thirty-five-year-old university assistant professor. One evening she worked late in her office, 10:30 p.m., and decided to walk from her building to the nearby parking lot by herself. This practice was discouraged by the university, and all Dorothy had to do was call the switchboard, and within ten minutes, she would have an escort. But she was tired and didn't want to wait those extra minutes.

Dorothy was only twenty feet from her building when an assailant jumped from behind some shrubbery, hit her on the head, rendering her semiconscious, and proceeded to rape her.

For the next six months, Dorothy dealt with her trauma with the help of a devoted and understanding fiancé, an effective counselor, and trusting, supportive friends and colleagues. Her adjustment to the event was excellent. Her earlier symptoms of PTSD—nightmares, anxiety attacks, fear of strangers, and mild occasional episodes of panic—subsided, and she had returned to her normal routine. With one exception: She never worked in her office after dark.

When asked how she was doing, Dorothy replied, "Great. I've put the trauma behind me. It's like it never happened. I don't think about it, and I've moved on." Most folks would say, "Good for you, Dorothy. You've put it behind you."

However, we detect a problem in Dorothy's reaction to her recovery, and it's shown in her comment "It's like it never happened." Yes, it's true, she is really doing fine, but there's an element of denial in those words, and denial of the past is not what is meant by "moving on."

Here's the problem: The event *did* happen. If Dorothy has denied in her mind that the event never really happened, she has left herself vulnerable. As one example, note that she never works in her office after dark. Sure, this move may seem wise, but consider that she has allowed the event to compromise her actions and limit her to what she can do after dark. For instance, if there is a departmental meeting in the early evening that will last until after dark, she skips it because she has not confronted and resolved a painful part of her reality.

Moving on does not mean that you cope best when you put an unpleasant event behind you, never again look at it, and reflect, "It's like it never happened." You cannot undo or rewrite the past. It happened; it's real. Following a traumatic event, sometimes that recognition, plus reflection on the past trauma, can help you put current challenges in perspective.

Rather than suppress memories of the trauma and act like it never occurred, a frank and realistic evaluation of the reality of the trauma can encourage Dorothy to be proactive and take some control. For example, she can work late in her office but call for an escort when she is ready to leave, she can take self-defense classes, and/or she can consider learning how to carry and use a weapon.

These actions should not be taken to give her a false sense of security but to give her feelings of self-empowerment and confidence. Thus "armed," both physically and psychologically, Dorothy will be more likely to make wise and realistic decisions to help her face the prospect of danger. The past *did* happen, and recognizing that fact will help Dorothy remain vigilant, proactive, and empowered in the future to take actions to control those things she can.

Putting trauma "behind you as if it never happened" carries two dangers: First, it makes you vulnerable to self-pity, the feeling that the corners of your world should be padded because you suffered the trauma. Second, you become vulnerable to self-blame. Dorothy, for instance, must not let the past dominate her thinking; she must not feel that others should join her pity parade. Nor should she beat herself up and moan, "Why didn't I do things differently?" Such obsessive thinking is dangerous and will interfere with effective coping in the present. In Dorothy's case, both self-pity and self-blame will hinder her proactive efforts to exercise some control in her life.

"Moving on" means not letting earlier conflict and trauma define you. It means remaining vigilant and being able to recognize the forces responsible for the conflict and trauma so you can deal with those forces as a rational, critical thinking, civilized adult. It means putting the past trauma in a box, wrapping it up, and placing it on a shelf in your mind.

Placed on that shelf, the event can now collect dust in the corner of your mind. However, it is always there, in sight, but situated so it doesn't dominate your thinking or define you. So you move on, knowing full well that the event happened but also knowing that you will not allow it to consume you by monopolizing your life.

<> <> <>

ROBYN THOUGHT SHE MOVED ON

When Robyn was a first-year college student, she became romantically involved with a senior. The relationship began OK and provided Robyn with security as she began the often-stressful first year in college. After a few months, however, things soured. The boyfriend became overly controlling and emotionally abusive. Robyn felt trapped by this guy who seemed to exert absolute control over her.

Robyn nearly transferred at the end of her first semester, but she stuck it out with the help of her roommate and some good friends. "I'll transfer this summer," she figured. The guy graduated at the end of year and disappeared from her life. Robyn had served his purpose. Over the summer, she opened up about the painful relationship to her parents and some former high-school friends at home. With everyone's help, she decided not to transfer. She liked her major, the professors, and many other aspects of her college life. Besides, her tormentor was gone.

Robyn graduated with honors and began what turned out to be a successful career with a small company. As far as she was concerned, the anxiety and stress of her first year in college was gone forever. She had moved on.

In her mid-thirties, she met Steve, thirty-six, and they became romantically involved. She began to believe that Steve was "the one," except for one part of him that made her uncomfortable: He loved doing things for her. He always insisted on picking up the check, he liked to do the driving, and he liked to be in charge of making plans, reservations, and other small day-to-day things.

One day Robyn confided to her old college roommate, "He's such a great guy, but I'm getting really anxious about the way he wants to be in charge. I know he's doing it because he loves me, but it scares me, and I don't know why. I love this guy so much, but I'm feeling trapped, overwhelmed. I'm suffocating. Sometimes I feel like I'm going to go into a complete panic, and I want to scream! I'm thinking of breaking it off."

Her friend, who was now a counseling psychologist, almost laughed. "My god, Robyn, don't you see that he reminds you of that f****r in college who ran your life into the ground? Yeah, Steve means well, but he's triggering all the anxiety you suffered when that a**hole was running your life! I was there! That s**t nearly destroyed you. My god, you have to talk to Steve and let him know that you can't have him doing everything for you, that he has to treat you like an equal or the relationship won't work!"

Robyn long ago thought she had "moved on." She didn't realize that the emotional residue from her trauma of years ago wasn't gone; it was merely dormant, latent, lying just below the surface of her conscious mind, ready to pounce when prompted. Steve's well-intentioned actions served as that prompt, and the fears and anxieties of being emotionally enslaved by her college boyfriend were reawakened in her mind.

Robyn took her friend's advice and took responsibility for initiating a frank talk with Steve. "Listen, Steve, if we're going to make a go of this relationship, we need to talk some things through." They talked everything over, were honest with each other, and discovered new things about each other.

Steve, for instance, was insecure in the relationship and felt if he didn't shower Robyn with love, she would dump him. Robyn explained how those actions apparently brought back the traumatic issues of seventeen years earlier. They both saw the need to allow each other to be autonomous and independent partners in the relationship and moved their bond to a deeper level of understanding. Robyn's friend was maid of honor a year later.

<>   <>   <>

COPING WITH DISAPPOINTMENT

During the corona pandemic, I [CB] was taking a walk and saw four young people in the park, each wearing their graduation cap and gown. They were laughing and having a great time as they posed for pictures taken by each of them in turn.

I wasn't sure what high school they had attended, but it didn't matter because every school in the area had canceled graduation exercises because of the coronavirus. But these four kids were doing a great job of coping with what had to be a disappointing time for them. Good for them!

Hara Estroff Marano wrote about the high school class of 2020 in *Psychology Today* (August 2020). Marano said these kids have been thrown a wicked curveball by life, a pitch that deprived them of a ceremony signaling achievement and filled with accolades and pride. "Life needs such events," said Marano. "Taking the time to acknowledge them . . . works as a kind of push-off to the challenges ahead. The future feels less certain, rockier, without the landmarks."

I imagined myself spouting this stuff to the four students in their graduation garb and just began laughing. Their future will be rougher without experiencing a ceremony? Nonsense! You know what I think? I think years down the road, those kids will have kids of their own, and one day their kids will suffer a terrible disappointment, and the parent will take them aside to comfort them.

"You think you have it bad? Let me tell you what happened when I graduated from high school 2020!" They will wear the graduation cancelation as a kind of badge of honor, kind of like when our grandparents tell us how they walked five miles to school each day, usually in a foot or two of snow.

As I continued walking, I began to think about how we cope or not cope with disappointment. Life is full of disappointments, beginning when we discover that we may not get fed before those hunger pangs begin, or we may not get a clean diaper right away. Then we reach that age when we can walk, and we long to discover all the wondrous things surrounding us, only to learn that the most frequently-used word in the language is "NO!"

In my forty-one years of teaching and advising college students, I had numerous office visits from students—not to talk about coursework, but to talk about some disappointment in their lives: broken romances, family finances that may preclude their return to college next year, alcohol/drug problems, acquaintance rape, sexual identity, roommate problems, parents trying to dictate their life, etc.

Disappointments happen. How many women have to cancel wedding plans fairly close to the ceremony? Maybe the guy gets cold feet and backs out. What could you do about it? No much, that's for sure. You have to accept the reality of the situation as best you can and solve the problems that arise as a result of the cancellation: notifying guests, returning gifts (should you?), canceling the honeymoon or taking the honeymoon with your bridesmaid.

No matter what the issue, my comments to "disappointed" students generally followed this model: Let them monopolize the conversation. Show understanding and empathy, not criticism. Ask them to identify what aspects of the situation they had some control over; ask them to identify what options—realistic ones—they had to solve the issue. In a few cases, I needed to refer them to my coauthor, or to the counseling center, or to an outside mental health service.

Most of the time, however, to one degree or another, they began to solve their problem on their own. That's right. Most of the students just needed someone to listen to—not judge—them, to tell them they weren't weird feeling as they did and that they had options.

A lot of parents don't prepare their kids for disappointment. These parents seem to feel that the road to healthy self-esteem is paved with success experiences. Thus, they work hard to protect their kids from failure and guarantee success in all they do. Unfortunately, this childrearing strategy fails to teach children how to cope with the reality of failure and disappointment.

Children need to be taught about the two greatest impostors they will ever face: success and failure. Both are impostors because success will have them believe they are better than they are, and failure will have them believe they are worse than they are.

They must be taught that success comes from preparation and effort. Success is not guaranteed, however, and they must guard against entitlement: "I worked hard, so I should only expect success." Sorry, kid, that's not how life works. You work hard to increase your odds of success, not guarantee it. Accountability is always involved.

Likewise, kids must learn that failure does not mean they are worthless and to blame. They must be taught to accept the fact that failure provides learning opportunities. They may have set unrealistically high goals, or maybe they did not prepare appropriately. Whatever the case, they must learn that failure gives them information about where they need to improve so they can increase their chance of success in the future.

When parents structure their children's environment to make success easy, the children don't learn that success comes from preparation and effort and failure results from absence of these actions, they don't learn to evaluate how realistic their expectations are about their personal capabilities, nor do they learn the danger in assuming that someone will always be there to bail them out. In short, they don't learn honor.

And remember, these points apply to all of us, not just to kids. Your biggest coping enemy is when you try to avoid failure because then you will never learn to correct mistakes and improve. To cope well, you must be willing to improve by examining and accepting your failures, learning from them, and not simply avoiding them. It's really the honorable thing to do!

<>   <>   <>

EITHER-OR THINKING

Do you prefer simple, definitive answers to questions? Suppose you hear on the news about a man who lives in your town. A local business where this guy worked was losing money and was forced to lay off 50 percent of its workforce, and he was one of them. Over a period of months, his financial situation worsened. He was unable to find another job, and his unemployment benefits ran out. His ten-year-old son has a life-threatening illness that requires medication he can no longer afford. Desperate, our unemployed dad breaks into a pharmacy and steals the medicine. How should this man be punished?

Simple answer: He committed a felony and should go to trial. If found guilty, he should go to jail.

Complicated answer: If found guilty, he should receive a suspended sentence, with required community service, and the requirement that he continue to look for work. His unemployment benefits should be extended; the drug company should supply him with the medication and put him on an affordable payment plan once he is back at work. Other local businesses and neighbors should work to help this family financially until he is able to find a job.

If you like the simple answer and believe that life is really an either-or deal, the odds are that you're going to have some coping problems somewhere along the line. Why? Because you want life to be something it isn't: simple. You want things to be black or white, right or wrong. If something is right for you, it should be right for everyone, and everyone should see it as right. You have no tolerance for ambiguity, subtleties, nuance, or dissenting opinions.

> *Always wanting simple answers is a form of avoidance—*
> *avoidance of experiencing the stress of discovering that*
> *what you believe doesn't hold up.*

Let's face it. Stress results when the answers to problems are not simple. It results when others disagree with you and don't see your way as best; it results when others show creativity, independence, and initiative. When faced with these situations, coping requires acceptance of other points of view, a willingness to compromise, respect and courtesy toward others—in short, coping requires honorable actions.

If you insist on living by simplistic, either-or, black-white rules, you will not be equipped to solve the challenges posed by complexities, shades of gray, and nuance. If you believe "there's only one way to solve this conflict," you will likely fail, and stress will continue to haunt you.

In chapter 1, we described Gene, who was tormented by inner insecurities resulting from fears of failure, rejection, and abandonment that had been instilled in him by his authoritarian father. This man believed children should be obedient, respectful, well-mannered, and hard-working. Anything short of perfection in the child was subject to criticism.

Gene's father embodies the either-or style of thinking we are describing: simplistic, black or white, right or wrong. There is no middle ground, no subtlety, no gray areas in this type of thinking. There is a right way of doing things, it is right for everyone, and everyone should see it as right for them. Alternatives are to be rejected not accepted.

Authoritarian thinking is counterproductive when it comes to effective coping and finding your honorable self.

Gene grew into adulthood filled with insecurities that forced him into the ego defense of *reaction formation*—we talked about this defense in the story of Karla and Tara in chapter 1. His father's excessive demands forced him into avoidance actions. His unconscious mind operated according to one principle: "I must avoid stress and conflict because I am unable to cope with them."

In 2020, at the height of the pandemic, people took to the streets to demonstrate against stay-at-home restrictions. Many TV viewers watched, fearful for their health if reopening occurred too soon, yet also empathetic with the demonstrators, understanding their psychological pain. Stress was in ample supply all around.

A major contribution to everyone's stress resulted from the either-or manner in which choices were delivered to the people: close or reopen society; follow the president or the governor; think like a liberal or a conservative; consider the medical or the financial aspects of the crisis; choose us or them, your needs or your neighbor's.

Again, we see that such either-or thinking is just too simplistic and encourages you to overlook the complexities of a problem, which makes coping difficult. Most conflicts are complex and subtle: "Should I assign Pete or Joan to lead the project team?" When you see the issue as either-or, Pete or Joan, you are putting yourself in a decision-making straitjacket that is almost guaranteed to maintain your stress level, no matter what you do.

Give yourself a break. Why not assign Pete and Joan as coleaders? If one obviously shines, you slowly elevate that one to leader. Notice how you have removed the either-or stressor and made the conflict data-driven: "I will let their performance determine which one emerges as leader."

> *As a general rule, to mitigate your stress over a conflict,*
> *change your thinking from "choose A or B" to "pick the*
> *best features from each choice."*

Assigning Pete and Joan as coleaders is a middle-ground solution. Then you can design your plan of action around that middle ground and continually measure (test) how well the plan is proceeding. The resolutions to most conflicts are usually most successful when they include features from all possible options and allow for feedback (data) to evaluate their effectiveness. Let Pete's and Joan's performance determine the final decision.

Note how this strategy makes your accountability much easier. You are guided by results, not by a gut feeling. You take responsibility for a course of action that has been tested.

<>   <>   <>

FINAL THOUGHTS

Accepting negative thoughts and feelings as a natural part of life will help you be less self-critical and upset with your life, especially if you believe you don't match up with your own and society's ideals. You're not weird or abnormal just because you experience troubling thoughts or feelings, and you're not here to live up to others' expectations.

So stop treating your emotions as if they are alien invaders. They are you! We all have them, and it's natural. You are not weird. Accept your emotions, but do not be governed by them. Acceptance of their presence and moving along in spite of their presence is good coping; letting emotions dominate you to the point that you struggle to deny them is not so good.

There are also times you must accept your pain without giving into tendencies to engage in some form of escape or avoidance that cause you to run from stress. Denial of what's going on in your life—drug/alcohol abuse, social withdrawal, gambling, eating disorders, or other acts of escape and avoidance—is likely to magnify and expand problems while taking you farther from your value systems.

If you value yourself and the roles you play in life—roles like parent, spouse, employee, or friend—but at the same time let yourself become less effective in these roles, how can you expect to feel better about yourself? Act honorably—with sincere commitment and dedication—toward those things you value in life.

As we said at the beginning of this chapter, keep in mind that acceptance does not refer to actions like giving up and quitting. Those actions signify weakness. Quite to the contrary, in the context of exercising your honorable self to cope with stress, accepting is the opposite of denial. When you deny the reality of the situation you are in and the emotions you feel, you are surrendering to your stress.

Acceptance, on the other hand, will grant you feelings of empowerment to confront and challenge situations that bring you painful emotions. The key is to focus on things under your control. You generally have no control over events or other people who bring you emotional distress. You do, however, have control over your thoughts and the actions you can perform to make those emotions work for you, not against you.

Growing to accept yourself and your emotions is a process, a way of living and interacting with others. It takes preparation, practice, effort, persistence, and endurance. It is not necessarily easy. Acceptance grows out of a type of thinking and acting that focuses on being realistic, not irrational. It emerges from facing your conflicts and anxieties, not avoiding them. It is based on positive and realistic actions and thoughts.

Perhaps, most of all, acceptance is based on a personal system of values and standards that provide you with a social conscience and give your life purpose and meaning. Your values give you the ability to act independently and honorably and result in actions and thoughts that will provide you with a sense of satisfaction and productivity.

CHAPTER 3

ACCOUNTABILITY

If we asked people to tell us what the word "accountable" means to them, most would probably say something like "taking responsibility for your mistakes. When things go wrong and it's your fault, you need to step up and say, 'It's on me.'"

We agree that being accountable means taking responsibility when you're the cause of things going wrong. But in the context of coping with stress, accountability is much more than admitting "I blew it." Accountable also means having the *courage* to accept the reality of what's going on in your life, it means having the *confidence* to empower yourself to take action to better your life, it means having a *willingness* to admit that you are not the center of it all, and finally, it means recognizing that the *needs of others* must play a role in the search for your honorable self.

DAVID FIGHTS CANCER

This story is the one exception to our statement in the preface that all the examples in this book are fabricated and involve fictitious people. David, not his real name, wrote this story for us, and with his consent, we included it in our book *Using Psychology to Cope with Everyday Stress*. David died a few months before this book went to press. With his widow's permission, we repeat his unedited letter as an example of several coping principles we talk about in this book and as a way to honor his memory.

> For almost eight years now [*It's 2016 when written*], I have been dealing with the fact that I have cancer. In December 2008, I came down with the flu or what I would describe as flu-like symptoms. Both my glands on my neck swelled and were very sore. After several weeks I regained my health but the gland on my right side of my neck never returned to its normal size.
>
> In March 2009, I received an email from a former girlfriend whom I had not had contact with since I was a teenager. We spent hours on the phone rekindling our relationship which began some 32 years earlier. I made the decision to relocate to where she was living. Four months later we were married and have been inseparable ever since. She has been my sunshine helping me cope.
>
> The growth on my neck kept getting bigger. In 2011, I decided to go to an ear, nose and throat doctor who also performs head and neck surgery. I had several tests run and the doctor said, "It's malignant." My heart dropped.
>
> The doctor explained treatments for the cancer: Another test, then surgery, radiation and chemotherapy. He said, "I may have to remove a portion of your tongue, voice box, and part of the jaw bone. You will have to learn to eat and speak again. You're looking at a possible five-year life expectancy."
>
> I gave myself a few days to talk things over with my wife and mull over the doctor's words. The bottom line was and is acceptance of the fact that I have been diagnosed with a malignant form of cancer. With the full support of my wife, I decided I would not undergo surgery, radiation or chemotherapy. I did attempt to

have only the tumor removed without undergoing the other treatments, but no doctor I contacted would consider doing so due to liability.

I emailed the doctor I originally received my diagnosis from and informed him I had chosen not to undergo cancer treatment. I received an email from him, telling me that without treatment, I had about three months to live. I did not respond and it only made me more determined to pursue other forms of treatment.

Over the 8 years since being first diagnosed, I have undergone several forms of alternative medicine treatments. There are many different forms of treatments available outside the U.S., but the cost, time away from work, travel, and treatment, make these unattainable for most.

I take a daily regimen of supplements (thanks to my wife), exercise and try to keep stress in my life minimal. Up until a few months ago, I was working sixty-three hours a week. I have reduced the number of hours to forty per week in order to pursue other personal interests. Whether or not any or all of this has contributed to beating the statistical odds, I do not know. What I do know is I am still here and living as normal a life as I did prior to the diagnosis. In fact, in a very real sense, I feel more alive than I did then. I don't take life for granted, but enjoy each and every moment of life and the good measure of health I have been blessed with on this day.

Some thoughts from me on my coping with everyday life—

1. Faith in God. I know not what tomorrow holds, but I know who holds tomorrow. God knows my life and nothing comes to me that does not first go through

Him. I'm not seeking a miracle healing, though I desire to be healed in this life, but if healing doesn't come, God is still God, and I will return to Him.

2. Connections between people and not possessions are what matters most.

3. Having an attitude of gratitude, thanksgiving, appreciation and forgiveness.

4. There is a song by Randy Stonehill. The lyrics state, "I'm gonna celebrate this heartbeat, because it just might be my last. Every day is a gift from the Lord on high, and they all go by so fast."

5. The only difference between my life and another is that I may know what I will die from. I say may because not even this is a guarantee.

6. The only things I have control over are my thoughts— what I believe—and my actions—what I do and how I respond based upon what I believe. Beyond that, things are beyond my control. It is enough. *(David died four years after writing this.)*

We're sure many readers know someone like David. Faced with the brutal reality of a devasting illness, they must choose how they want to attack the illness. That choice, of course, can also change as time and circumstances change. There are people who fight cancer with radiation and chemo for an extended period, then have times of remission, only to have the cancer return years later. Like David, when given the choice of renewed treatment, many say, "No. That's it. No more. I can't take it anymore. I don't care if you tell me I'll be dead in a month, I'm going to spend that month with some quality of life, not puking in a bucket."

In a sense, that's what David did. He accepted his situation, took control, and became accountable for making a decision. He lived on his own terms, rebuilding and enjoying twelve years of life. He coped—and died—with honor.

<> <> <>

IDENTITY IN THE WORKPLACE

In 2020, pandemic "stay-at-home" policies stretched into weeks, and the psychological and financial strains on those who were unable to work brought many to the breaking point. They took to the streets to demonstrate their frustration and displeasure.

From a coping context, one's work is obviously a source of financial security. Being unemployed, even if only for a few weeks, can create financial havoc for a family. Unemployed workers struggle to hang on to their sanity, even though circumstances prevent them from fulfilling their purpose, their obligation to their families.

Employment can also be a source of psychological stability. Being able to work is a strong psychological component of one's identity. Those who bring home a paycheck are able to look in the mirror and see someone who is responsible, productive, and capable of caring for others. "I am the breadwinner for my family. They depend on me for food and shelter. It's my responsibility to take care of them, and I am meeting that responsibility." When a job is taken away, those traits— those essential parts of a healthy view of self—are taken away. The result can be psychological devastation, a literal disintegration of the personality.

Many workers also develop intense loyalty to their place of employment, and the workplace becomes an extension of self-identity, "who I am." Unemployment can be a vital threat to that sense of identity and make a worker feel lost, abandoned, and rejected. Those feelings can make an individual extremely vulnerable to mental illness.

Let's look at this aspect of employment—a component of one's identity—a little more closely. Doing so can shed light on how one's career and workplace can be a source of stress that makes coping with life very hard.

We have known students who, during their senior year of college, express concern about their postgraduation plans. Lenny's hypothetical case represents the issue:

I majored in psychology because it was a good, general undergrad major that applied to a lot of areas. I never really wanted to work in the field, but now I do. This stuff turns me on, and I really want to use it and help people. I'm looking to get a master's in counseling and get licensed. The problem is my dad wants me to join the family business after graduation. We always talked about this, and I thought it would work, but now I think differently. I spent last summer working with him, and I realized that this was not what I wanted to do. The work I would be doing with Dad is just not who I am. Any advice on how to tell him?

That's a tough question. Lenny needs to be true to himself, of course, and in cases like this, most dads, even though disappointed, will eventually see that letting his son go "his chosen way" is in the son's best interests. Maybe Lenny should take time over the summer to give working with Dad a trial run. He could see what's involved and if he likes it. If not, he can honestly say, "It's not for me, Dad." Furthermore, Lenny can be reassured that he need not fear his dad saying, "Well, you could have at least given the family business a go." He did! Also, Lenny need not worry going through life wondering, "What would have happened if . . . ?" Once again, he can say, "I gave it a try, and I know it's not for me."

Trevor is business-administration major and an academic superstar. After college, he landed a great job with a major company. He seemed well on his way to a rewarding and lucrative professional career.

After two years on the job, he contacted one of his college professors and said, "I'm doing really well. Great evaluations from the boss, already two raises, colleagues I enjoy working with—"

The professor interrupted. "Sounds like a 'but' is coming!"

Trevor laughed. "Yeah, a big 'but.' The company culture doesn't fit with my values. Bottom line, bottom line, bottom line—always the bottom line. I read spreadsheets showing budget reductions requiring employee termination, and I think, who are these people? Do they have kids? A mortgage? College loans to repay? I just can't get away from the people angle. It's more important to me than the bottom line."

"So what are you planning to do?" asked the professor.

"Nursing school. I'm going to be a dentist," replied Trevor.

"Wow! That's quite a career change!"

Trevor's choice is not as wild as it sounds. For years, he had suffered from multiple sclerosis and had undergone various treatments from various physicians. He was always interested in medicine. The problem with his delayed choice at this point in time, however, was that he had taken none of the science courses required for admission to nursing school.

He discovered that the university where he lived had a nursing school and also a special program where he could take a concentrated and intense year-and-a-half of biology, chemistry, and physics to give him the requisite courses to apply to nursing school.

Would you agree that this would be a gutsy move on Trevor's part? Of course. If nothing else, he would show himself to be willing to take on the challenge because he didn't want to go through life wondering, "What if . . . ?"

Three situations: unemployment, choosing against family wishes, making a radical career change. What might they have in common? Several things, perhaps, but definitely *accountability*. The unemployed worker must take responsibility for meeting this challenge by filing for unemployment compensation, looking for other sources of income, and helping the family maintain its stability. Lenny must be responsible for respectfully and lovingly communicating his decision to his dad. Trevor must meet the conditions put on him if he is to be successful in carrying out her revised career plans.

EMOTIONAL INTELLIGENCE

Intelligence—if you're like most people, when you run across this word, you think of cognitive skills: a good memory, large vocabulary, math ability, reading comprehension, and critical-thinking skills. In general, you probably think of an intelligent person as someone who has a lot of knowledge in a variety of areas.

You probably don't think of an intelligent person as one who is necessarily good at coping with stress. Would you find the following comment contradictory? "Jim is one of the most intelligent guys I know, but he sure doesn't know how to handle conflicts with others or how to deal with anxiety! Put him in a stressful situation and he falls apart." No contradiction at all, right?

Intuitively, most people separate cognitive abilities and coping abilities; cognitive deals with knowledge, coping deals with emotions. In fact, in a 1964 paper, psychologists Davitz and Beldoch talked about *emotional intelligence* as different from *cognitive intelligence*. They linked the latter to cognitive abilities but tied the former to effectiveness in social communication, especially the ability to empathize with others.

Let's use the term *emotional intelligence* to describe those who are "secure in their own skin." They have healthy levels of self-esteem and feel empowered to be autonomous, independent, confident, and optimistic as they confront the challenges of daily life. Individuals with high emotional intelligence are good at accepting reality, taking responsibility for their actions, setting priorities, and navigating their way through the maze of stressors that regularly confront them.

Sounds good, but emotional intelligence is not the whole story when it comes to coping effectively with stress. Many people high in emotional intelligence appear to be pretty confident and secure, at least on the outside, as they tend to their needs. Unfortunately, they may leave a trail of human psychological carnage in their wake if they focus on an egotistical coping strategy that puts them at the center of it all. In their own minds, they are coping well, but they do so with a lot of deception, manipulation, lying, cheating, and bullying.

What we're saying is emotional intelligence by itself is no guarantee of effectively coping with stress. If that's true, we have to ask, "What's missing? What else is needed to use emotional intelligence to cope in positive ways?" The answer to that question involves an intelligence that supplements emotional: *moral intelligence*.

*Coping with everyday life will be most effective when
emotional intelligence is complemented by moral
intelligence.*

How would we describe people with a healthy moral intelligence?
They have values, standards, and a social conscience, which means they
weigh their coping actions against the needs of others.

Peter says, "Embezzling money may be good for me financially, but
others are going to suffer, so I choose not to embezzle."

We say, "Peter has moral intelligence!"

*If you have low moral intelligence, if you do not value
others as dignified and worthy of courtesy and respect,
you will have no problem cheating and manipulating
them to satisfy your own greed. How dishonorable!*

Moral intelligence means having empathy for others, being able to
understand how they are feeling. Here's another statement from Peter
that shows high moral intelligence: "If I insult and disparage others in
the presence of their children, I may feel good, but I also show my total
disregard for the pain I inflict on their offspring. As much as I dislike
them, I will not disrespect them in the presence of their family."

Here's what we're saying: You may have high *emotional intelligence* and
feel really great about yourself. But if you have low *moral intelligence* and can
only focus on you, if you must include yourself as the primary ingredient
in your life coping recipe, ultimately, your coping efforts will fail because
you will leave behind a legacy of making others feel badly about themselves.
Your legacy will be others who scowl at the very mention of your name.

Both emotional and moral intelligence are essential components to
the honorable self. You simply cannot and will not cope well without
those aspects of honor, an honor that gives you insight into your
emotional life and that provides you with a moral compass that gives
you both direction and compassion.

<> <> <>

RATIONALIZATION

Did you ever give an excuse for a mistake you made? Of course, you did—we all do it.

Your spouse asks, "Why are you late?" You say, "The traffic was insane." (What you should have said: "I lost track of time and was late leaving to get you. Sorry. I blew it. Next time, I'll leave earlier.")

Your boss says, "You're the project team leader, and I have to say the proposal you presented leaves a lot to be desired." You say, "Some of the team members just dropped the ball and didn't tell me." (What you should have said: "I didn't monitor the team on a daily basis to make sure we were on schedule. At the last minute, I had to throw stuff together to get the report in on time. I'm to blame. If you'll give me an extension, I will personally correct the flaws.")

In the examples above, the "you say" excuses are a poor way to cope. They are pure avoidance of accountability, plain and simple. Sure, you may temporarily escape some direct criticism from others, but in the long run, you have made yourself vulnerable to doubts from others: "Is he reliable? Can I really depend on him to be on time?" "Does she really have the leadership skills to run a team? Should I replace her?"

On the other hand, the "what you should say" responses show excellent coping. First, you take responsibility and admit fault. Second, you say you know why you're at fault. Third, you ask for a chance to demonstrate how you will correct your mistake. These steps are the essence of good coping: *acceptance* of your actions, *accountability* for the outcome, a *correction plan* for the future.

Obviously, when things go wrong, it is not always your fault. But if you get in a chronic, habitual pattern of making excuses when you fail, you are using the ego defense of rationalization. When confronted with failure, your default mode does not include taking blame for it or apologizing—"I am responsible for this mess, and I apologize for it." This phrase is simply not in your vocabulary.

What does excessive use of rationalization say about you? You are insecure about your ability to handle challenges. You have a fear of failure. Your self-esteem is low. You experience feelings of helplessness and incompetence when faced with an obstacle.

Using rationalization shows weak ego strength, insecurities that must be hidden from both others and yourself.

Faced with failure, without excuses your fragile ego, which cannot handle failure, will crumble, and you will be plunged into anxiety. You must, therefore, avoid facing the possibility that you are responsible for the failure by making excuses to deflect the blame elsewhere.

The solution to your problem is not difficult, and involves three steps. First of all, step one, you need to determine how often you make excuses for a mistake. Remember, what we have just said refers to excessive, chronic rationalization. You will have coping issues if your standard reaction to making a mistake is to blame something or someone else for your error. If your evaluation of your tendency to put fault elsewhere is extreme – meaning you do it almost all the time – it's time for step two.

Step two involves analyzing your mistakes carefully and objectively. Let's suppose your car is rear-ended while you are sitting at a traffic light, which is still red when the collision occurs. You say to the investigating officers, "It wasn't my fault. The light was still red and this guy wasn't paying attention and he plowed right into me! I'm not to blame." Fortunately for you, two witnesses verify your story. They were standing at the intersection waiting for the light to turn when the crash occurred.

Note that in this case, when you say it was the other guy's fault you are not rationalizing; you are being completely accurate in assigning blame for the accident. But what if things were different? You say to the officer, "It wasn't my fault. The light was still red and this guy wasn't paying attention and he plowed right into me! I'm not to blame."

Unfortunately, the two witnesses say, "The light had turned green and we were halfway across the street. The driver who was hit [that's you!] was not paying attention and just stayed at the light. The other guy saw the green light and thought the car in front was moving until it was too late." In this case, when you assign blame to the other driver, you are rationalizing because you can't face the fact that your mind was elsewhere and you caused the accident. Time for step three.

Step three is when you teach yourself to move away from rationalization. How? You must accept the reality of the situation and take responsibility for what happened. "I was not focused on the conditions and I am responsible for what happened. After accepting the consequences of my mistake, I must take steps to make sure this situation is not likely to occur again." In other words, you must correct your mistakes.

Imagine a football coach who is asked, "Well, coach, your team was really outplayed today. What happened?" He replies, "What happened? Did you see the officiating? How could we possibly win this game when the refs were obviously biased against us? They made terrible calls that cost us the game?" Given such rationalization, is the coach likely to work with the team to correct the mistakes they made that cost them the game? No.

When you analyze your car accident and accept the fact that it was clearly your fault, in step three you assess what you did wrong and take steps to correct your errors. "I remember now. I took a bite of my sandwich and some of it fell on the floor. I reached down to pick it up and the collision occurred." Solution? No more eating in the car; no more retrieving dropped objects unless you're in a parking space or your driveway.

The point here is simple: Rationalization is an avoidance strategy to free you from having to face your errors, a strategy based on the faulty belief that your mistakes are character flaws. In fact, your mistakes actually present opportunities for self-improvement. So, you might as well *accept* them as a part of life, make yourself *accountable* in facing them, and develop a *rational plan* to cope with them. Sounds pretty empowering, doesn't it? Make these character-driven traits a part of an *honorable* approach to life and you will reap unexpected benefits.

<>   <>   <>

SELF-EXAMINATION

A lot of stress is self-inflicted, especially in interactions with others. How often do you say or do something that produces negative reactions, such as anger, in others? How often do you consider the possibility that you, not the other person, caused the problem? Probably not too often, right?

Here's a tip for dealing with social conflict that increases your stress: Be willing to accept some responsibility for being the cause of the conflict. This is not a comfortable process because to pull it off, you must look inward and objectively examine your values, social conscience, and life purposes.

> *You must ask yourself, "How do I define myself? Are my actions consistent with my self-definition, with who I believe I am?"*

Notice how these types of questions combine accountability with an examination of your honorable self.

> *Self-examination is fine, but it is only after you put accountability in that examination that you will move toward self-discovery and self-development. Without that combination, self-examination runs the risk of excessive self-criticism—which leads to self-blame, feeling unworthy, helplessness, and vulnerability to depression.*

Only by asking questions in the context of honor will you be able to deal with negative reactions like anger, either coming from you or from another, in assertive but respectful ways. Only then can you see that the anger in others may be justified. By the same token, only then can others possibly see your anger as justified. Social interactions are always a two-way street.

Without the honest self-examination, you're likely to meet anger with anger, resort to profane and childish insults, and cast blame on the other party. Then the other person will judge you as selfish, weak, defensive, and immature.

If you define yourself by your negative emotions—your anger, anxieties, fear, and sanctimony—you are on a self-defeating road. Effective coping requires you to apply your values and standards to your emotional roles and actions as spouse, parent, friend, coworker, son/daughter, etc. You must determine if your actions in these roles are consistent with your conscience and purpose. If not, you must work to correct the inconsistencies.

<>   <>   <>

THE "WHY?" QUESTION

Dean challenges Barb with a question: "Why do you feel so strongly about that? Your position is totally illogical!"

Later, Barb finds herself ruminating on the exchange with Dean. "Why do I feel so strongly about it? Am I being unreasonable? Am I illogical? My position makes sense to me, and I'm totally comfortable with it, but maybe Dean is right. Maybe I should change my opinion."

Students have often told us, "You know what I hate? Having someone ask me why I do something! 'Why do you get up so early? You should sleep in.' 'You don't want to go out tonight? Why not? It's Friday.' Or I'm sitting in the cafeteria with some guys, and one of them says, 'Why do you mix your peas in with your mashed potatoes? That's gross!'

"I mean, why do people care when I get up, or how I eat, or that I have to be in a party mood when they are? Can't I live my life the way I want to? Am I here to please them or to do things the way I like?"

That last question really says it all and gets to the heart of the issue: You really aren't here to live up to the expectations of others, and they are not here to live up to yours. Each of us has a responsibility to be authentic and true to ourselves.

Will you be satisfied with your life if you try to be someone you are not, someone another person insists you be? If you agree that the answer to that question is "no," it will be easier for you to resist pressure to be what others want you to be. You will feel more personally authentic, accountable, and be better able to work through the down times.

Let's return to Barb's dilemma. She's wondering why she gets so bent out of shape when her friend criticizes her for being disagreeable. "Is Dean right?" she asks. "Do I need to see things his way?"

When confronting your emotions, does asking yourself "Why do I feel this way?" automatically produce insight and growth? Let's face it. Most people go into counseling seeking an answer to why questions: "Why I am feeling this way? Why do I have these negative emotions? Why do I get so anxious around others? Why can't I be more decisive?" Is posing these questions, like Barb does after her argument with Dean, always a good thing?

Common sense says trying to answer those questions honestly should lead to greater insight, learning, understanding, and positive growth. That may be true to some extent, but some research finds that *excessive focusing* on "why" questions can be unproductive and even harmful.

Ethan Kross of Columbia University asked undergraduate students to recall an experience when they felt intense anger toward someone. One group was told to vividly reflect on the experience in their minds; another group was told to imagine they were simply an observer watching themselves get angry at the other person. Only students in the second group showed lower anger when thinking about the original experience. The students who were encouraged to dwell on their anger actually got angrier.

Here's the coping lesson in this research: Dwelling on "Why do I feel this way?" is not always effective because you are focusing on the emotion and the person who aroused the emotion in you. Instead, you must view yourself more objectively, not as a victim of the emotion but as someone who can exercise some control over how you view your emotion. In a sense, you are reframing the problem from an emotion-based one to a problem-based one.

You must restructure your thinking about yourself—"I can control my thinking"—and others—"I cannot control what they say." Understanding that distinction is one thing that coping with honor means—realizing that control is something best exercised on yourself, not on others.

> *Positive growth requires posing not the question of "Why?" but posing the question of "What," as in "What can I do to develop thoughts and actions that bring me more personally satisfying outcomes?" Your focus should be on actions, not emotions.*

As we said in the previous section, the danger in the "why" question is that it leads to self-criticism, which makes you feel unworthy, which leads to helplessness, which leads to depression: "Why do I feel this way? I shouldn't feel this way. Something is wrong with me. What can I do about it? I don't know. Geez, what good am I anyway?"

Being accountable involves more than asking "why" something happened. Yes, that type of question is involved in the process of analyzing events and your role in them, but a complete analysis must proceed far beyond "why." In chapter 6, we will have much more to say about involving the "what" context in any accountability activity.

CHAPTER 4

HUMILITY

As you read this chapter, you will discover that, in the context of coping at least, it is difficult to discuss humility without venturing into the importance of empathy. In a very real sense, therefore, chapters 4 and 5 are interrelated, and chapter 4 establishes a foundation for chapter 5.

THE HUMILITY COPING CLOCK

Why would humility be an important part of coping effectively with stress? The answer is simple: Psychologically, humility involves much more than simply admitting your mistakes and weaknesses; much more than not allowing yourself to be an egotistical braggart when you do well. Yes, such actions are a helpful part of coping, but they serve you best when you allow what we call the *humility coping clock* to play to completion.

What exactly is the *humility coping clock*? Imagine a circular clock face. At the 12, noon, we place the words "Honorable Coping." That, of course, is our goal.

At 2 on the clock face, we write "Humility." Humility encourages you to admit that you should not be the primary ingredient in your life recipe. That is, life is not all about you; there are always others involved.

At 4, we write "Optimism." We believe that humility can help release you from your personal pity party, give you a sense of freedom that is uplifting, and instill you with an optimistic spirit.

Continuing the progression around the clock, we write "Sharing" at 6. Strengthened with your newfound optimism, you will be more likely to "share yourself" with others who are also fighting stress in their lives.

Sharing your struggles with others not only requires you to talk to them, but it also requires you to listen to and learn from them. In this way, the seeds of empathy are planted in your mind, and we write "Empathy" at 8.

That brings us to the final phase along the circle, the "Actions" that close out the day on the clock at 10. Talking to, listening to, and learning from others will inevitably show you the essence of effective coping: taking action in a context of optimistic empathy.

> *The clock is now complete. Can you see it? You begin with reducing a focus on yourself as the center of it all and end with an empathetic understanding of others who are wrestling with similar life challenges as you are. But now, released from the prison of a self-absorbed ego, you are able reach out to help others because you understand their plight. Purged of considering yourself special and deserving of pity, you cope with your stressors by helping others with their difficulties. And you also enjoy the benefits because you are participating in the fullness of the human experience.*

Read again in chapter 1 the hypothetical story of Kevin, the widower on disability. You will see the humility clock beautifully exhibited.

Many people have difficulty coping with stress because they make their problems all about them. Sounds contradictory, doesn't it? If you're all tied up in knots because of some obstacle life has thrown in your way, isn't your problem all about you? After all, you're the one feeling the stress.

Alex is at work, and she gets a call from her supervisor. "Alex, I've made a decision on assigning primary responsibility for that project you and Carl started working on. I've decided to go with Carl. He has more experience in this area, and I think he's the one who should carry the ball."

Alex was hoping she would get the nod, not Carl. She's devasted, angry, anxious—a whole array of emotions flood her. "Why Carl? Why not me? Am I on the way out? Don't they value me around here? Is it because I'm a woman? This really depresses me. I've been good to this company. What a lousy thing to do to me. God, this is just awful."

Me, me, me. I, I, I. Alex is one step away from forming her own pity parade because she has been wronged. She talks and thinks her way into becoming an emotional cripple. To say Alex is not coping well would be quite the understatement.

What's missing here in this coping challenge? What does Alex need to help her deal better with the stress of the rejection? Humility, of course.

Humility is an important part of coping effectively with stress because it involves much more than simply admitting your mistakes and weaknesses, much more than not allowing yourself to be an egotistical braggart when you do well. Sure, such actions are a helpful part of coping, but they serve you best when you allow humility to be a part of the *humility clock*. It is only then that your humility leads you to the ultimate coping process—interacting with others in a mutual empathetic interaction. We'll have more to say about that in chapter 5.

As for Alex? From a coping standpoint, the reality is there—Carl is in charge. She should make sure that Carl does not see her as a threat. She should go to him and say, "The boss said you're in charge. You can count on me to work hard on this thing and get it down on time. You will have my full cooperation."

COMPARING STRESS LEVELS

During the 2020 election campaign, we saw a tweet about Joe Biden, written by someone who had lost a child. The writer commented how he couldn't imagine Biden's pain from losing two children and a spouse. One other reply to the tweet was a little less sympathetic and said, "I've had it a lot worse than Biden, and so have most Americans."

Let's strip this exchange of all things political, and talk about coping with stress. Specifically, let's ask, "Does comparing the intensity of your stress with someone else's—"I have suffered more than you have"—help you cope better?"

Suppose you are in a support group to help you deal with some stressful event. You have just shared your story with the group and someone says, "Big deal. I've had it a lot tougher than you! You got off easy." Would you feel better after hearing their story? We would imagine not. No matter how intense their experience was, your trauma and pain do not simply go away.

Here's the thing: Being stressed out and needing help is not a competition. When you hear that someone else has problems that make yours look minor, you might be tempted to say to yourself, "Why am I getting so overwhelmed by this? Others have bigger problems than mine."

Maybe so, but if your life is being disrupted by this stress, you need to tend to the problem, or the stress will intensify and likely lead to worse difficulties. The degree to which stressful events affect you is not determined by how your stress stacks up against someone else's. And when you start comparing stress loads, you will feel shame and guilt if you decide someone else's issues are worse than yours. Any way you look at it, comparing stress intensities is a losing proposition.

Consider this question: When someone says, "I've had it a lot tougher than you," what is missing from their coping process? Two things, really: First is *humility*. As soon as someone says their road has been rockier than yours, they are descending into the depths of self-glorification; they are telling you, "I, not you, am the primary ingredient in the recipe we're dealing with here. It's all about me!"

When you remove humility from the coping picture, you won't be able to deal with your problems effectively. Imagine this exchange:

Jim: I lost my job, I can't sleep, I can't eat, I'm depressed, I don't know what to do!

Bill: Oh, for heaven's sake, give me a break. Try having your wife walk out on you with another guy and leave you with two kids to raise.

Jim: Well, if you still have your job, at least you can afford to feed them!

Bill: Young kids need their mother! I can't do that kind of parenting. I need help and don't know where to turn.

This is pretty absurd, isn't it? Both Jim and Bill are working very hard to convince the other that his burden is heavier. The fact is the burden is heavy for each of them, and both Jim and Bill need to address their respective problem.

In addition to humility, the second thing missing when stress loads are compared is the sprout of humility's seed: *empathy*. In the exchange above, for instance, neither speaker empathizes with the suffering of the other; they only feel their own discomfort. The result is that neither is able to resolve their stress.

The irony for Jim and Bill is that if they bothered to hear the other's story, they just might gain some insight into their own difficulty. When you're stressed and upset, you struggle to find ways to deal with emotions like fear, anxiety, guilt, grief, jealousy, and others that rob you of stability in your life. At this point in the coping process, you think it's all about you, and this self-centered emphasis makes coping difficult. Without humility, you can't move to the next position on the *humility clock*.

When you get outside of yourself, however, and bring others into the picture, the coping picture brightens. Whether you reach out to others with problems similar to yours, or work at trying to understand the effect you are having on others, substituting an "other-oriented," rather than "self-oriented," focus will provide insight into your problem. This focus is what we mean by empathy.

One final point to make about comparing stresses: Such a comparison is less likely when a victim is in a support group designed specifically for his or her difficulty. Thus, "Compassionate Friends" and "Healing Hearts" bring bereaved parents together. If the issue is divorce or separation, there are other support groups and different ones for women, men, those over forty, and even those with a specific religious affiliation. When you're with similar people who have experienced problems like yours, the issue of comparison is less likely to rear its ugly head.

<>   <>   <>

REFLECTIONS ON AN EMPTY GROCERY SHELF

I [CB] had seen it on news reports and heard about it from others. But when I went to the grocery store for the first time since the reality of the coronavirus was taking hold in the public mind, there it was: an empty grocery shelf in the section where paper products like toilet paper and tissues normally filled what was now vacant space. Over the next few days, and as I took more trips to the store, it occurred to me that the empty shelf carried some good coping messages.

The first thing that occurred to me was narcissism. The narcissist believes "It's all about me. I am the major ingredient in all life recipes. I am the crucial variable in the equation that will solve the problem."

Now I'm not saying that all the folks who grabbed armfuls of multipack TP are narcissists. No doubt some of them had large families at home and were replacing their dwindling stock of TP. I bet there were even some folks who saw the shelf getting depleted but had a decent supply at home and decided to leave the small remainder on the shelf for others. But for sure there were no doubt many who had a garage full of TP, considered themselves fortunate to have stumbled on even more, and scooped up TP like a squirrel hoarding nuts for the winter. The narcissist's mantra is "I deserve all I can get."

Narcissism encourages a "me versus them" orientation. If you're white, non-whites are the enemy; if you're a native-born American, immigrants and even naturalized citizens are the enemy; those who do not accept your beliefs are the enemy; those who would take "my TP" are the enemy. The pathetic narcissist has a lot of enemies and must constantly be on the defensive to avoid psychological collapse. What an inefficient way to cope with stress.

I also decided that the empty shelf symbolizes humility. When you lack humility, you form your own pity parade when things don't go your way. You wail about the unfairness of it all—"I deserve better!"—and talk and think your way into becoming an emotional cripple.

Reality, however, dictates that there are always others involved. If you *accept* that reality, you can embrace humility. You can free yourself from demanding pity from others and find empowerment and optimism. You can feel pride in your accomplishments, but understand that your successes do not grant you preferential treatment. This realization will make you more inclined to "share yourself" with others who are also fighting stress. Sharing is a powerful and productive strategy for coping with stress.

The empty shelf obviously shows the importance of empathy in the coping process. We'll say more about it in the next chapter, but empathy is not sympathy; it is a sensitivity that allows you to understand others in the context of their needs, not yours. As a result, you focus your actions around values, social conscience, and morality. This focus brings you honor and provides both giver (you) and taker (the other) many psychological benefits. There is no more effective therapy than empathetic service to others. Assist others along your life path, and you will never be alone.

"All this from an empty shelf?" you say. Why not? Let's personify that shelf and imagine a conversation with it.

> You: Hello, shelf. I must say you're looking a little depressed today.
>
> Shelf: How would you feel if your entire purpose in life has been taken from you? I am here to provide things to please people, but they have stripped me of everything I am and left me empty.

During a time of crisis, when we stand in front of the shelf that is stocked with items, our self-preservation kicks in. Screw the neighbor! Narcissism rules; humility and empathy are overpowered. We strip the shelf bare, and the shelf becomes us! Empty! Without honor!

For our common benefit, that outcome is what we must prevent. Crises that threaten our inner being can bring out the worst in us. "Think of your neighbor" morphs into "Everyone for themselves!"

You have to decide which one is you and act accordingly. Which action is consistent with your values, your character, your morality, your ethics? One thing for sure: Finding your honorable self—which in this context means discarding narcissism and embracing humility and empathy—will help you cope with any crisis. In the final analysis, that coping strategy—not one that stresses "It's all about me!"—is what life needs to be about.

POLITICAL CORRECTNESS

Every year it seems complaints about politically-correct language increase around holiday time. You know, the "happy holidays" versus "Merry Christmas" stuff. Those who whine about this issue seem to forget that PC language boils down to humility, courtesy, and respect for others who have a perspective different from theirs.

To one degree or another, we all see ourselves as the most important ingredient in our life. The strength of this self-serving bias varies from person to person and even within ourselves at different times. Any way you look at it, however, the bias is there, and it has the potential to make using PC language distasteful to those who refuse to accept that there's a world out there beyond their personal space.

Being conflicted about using PC language can be a source of stress in interpersonal relations. If you're one of those people who has issues with PC language, here's a coping thought: Soften your life recipe to acknowledge the importance of ingredients other than yourself. Ask yourself, "What determines how others remember me?" The answer is "People remember how you make them feel."

> *What sort of daily legacy do you want to leave? Do you*
> *want people to remember you as someone who makes*
> *them feel undervalued and inferior to you? Or do you*
> *want them to remember you as someone who makes*
> *them feel good because you understand and respect their*
> *perspective?*

Why not adopt a little *humility* and decide that life is not all about you? Why not take the time to make others feel worthy of your respect? Doing so will remove from your mind frivolous, nonsensical things like worrying about PC language. You will feel more empowered and independent, you will feel more productive, and those feelings will bring you more personal satisfaction. Most important, you'll have more pleasant interactions with others.

<>   <>   <>

COURTESY IS EMPOWERING

Todd and Sam were entering a restaurant. Todd went first just as a customer was leaving. Todd didn't give way to the exiting customer but continued ahead through the doorway, forcing the customer to step aside. Sam, however, directly behind Todd, stopped, stepped aside, and motioned to the customer to walk out before Sam entered.

Once inside, Todd said to Sam, "Why did you do that? Don't you know that by letting that guy out, you were basically telling him he was your superior? You backed down."

Incredulous, Sam replied, "What are you talking about? Being courteous shows you're secure, that letting someone else be first is not a threat to you. In fact, when you nearly pushed him out of the way, you were showing that you couldn't let a stranger have the upper hand. Sorry, buddy, but that shows insecurity."

What do you think? Who was showing the better coping skill, Todd or Sam? We believe it was Sam for the following reasons:

Many people seek a stress-free life with minimal unpleasant emotions. The problem is that approach makes them the essential part of the equation, where they see themselves as virtuous and entitled. This approach is selfish and will fail in the long run. When it comes to coping, what you want is not there lying on the ground to be picked up and put in your pocket.

When coping with stress, don't *seek* things from life; don't just wander around looking to pick up solutions to your problems. Rather, *participate* in life; *experience* it through actions. Experiencing life allows positive emotions to emerge from your actions. Consider, for example, the case of Todd and Sam, which really boils down to old-fashioned courtesy.

Polite actions put needs of another person in your coping equation. When you include others in the picture, you can feel some *humility* as you show yourself that others are important, and *empowerment*, as you see, you can participate with life in ways that will give you confidence. Don't *look for* emotions and feelings; allow yourself to *experience* them by acting in ways that don't make you the center of attention.

Todd needed to keep himself as the center of his actions, which is an ego-based strategy designed to protect a fragile sense of self. Sam, on the other hand, made the other person the focus; he showed himself that he was confident and secure within himself and empowered to act with a social conscience.

Think about it. When you feel all stressed out that your life is spiraling out of control, that you are suffocating, maybe you should find a little humility. Maybe you should accept the fact that you are not the be-all and end-all to all social situations. Maybe you should make yourself accountable for making others feel comfortable around you. Maybe you should allow yourself to bring the needs of others into the picture before you act.

DO YOU "MOLEST" YOUR RELATIONSHIPS?

When you hear words like "molester" and "abuser," you probably think of sexual or brutal physical attacks. In a very broad sense, however, the psychological dynamics that underlie the molester's and abuser's actions can also come into play in everyday relationships. When they do, the relationship is probably doomed to become a source of discomfort for all involved.

What we're suggesting is that some of the dynamics of the molester—insecurity, immaturity, narcissism, anxiety, fear of competition and losing that competition—are at work in many everyday relationships that are in trouble.

Think about any relationships that are causing you stress and anxiety. The problem could be with a friend, coworker, spouse, parent, child, or whomever. As a first step in helping you begin to confront the coping challenge and find actions that might help you move toward a resolution of the conflict, ask yourself some specific questions. As always, focus on the issue, not the emotion, and keep your questions within the boundaries of "What parts of this situation are under my control?" Be forewarned: Finding honest answers to these questions is going to require you to find some humility.

The most fundamental questions are:

> "Am I able to maintain my individuality, my sense of self, in my relationships with others?"
>
> "Can I share, cooperate, compromise, respect those who disagree with me, and even admit I'm wrong, but through it all remain myself?"
>
> "Am I secure in my own skin?"

These are tough questions requiring some honest self-assessment. The premise, however, says that if you want a truly meaningful relationship, you must be pretty firm in your sense of self.

Here are some other penetrating questions:

> "Do I subjugate myself to his/her will, or do I feel compelled to assert power and dominance?"
>
> "Do I feel in competition with him/her?"
>
> "Do I fear I will lose the competition?"

"Does (s)he arouse anxiety and insecurities in me?"

"Am I behaving in childish ways?" (If you can't relate to "childish," simply ask yourself if you deal with the person like you're on the playground during recess in the third grade!)

Asking such questions in the context of a specific relationship can lead you to broader questions:

"In general, can I work with others as someone who is stable and self-assured, or do I look for relationships to compensate for my weaknesses, insecurities, and dependency needs?"

"Do I constantly look for attention and approval from others?"

"Do I suffocate others with demands, possessiveness, and jealousy, trying to make them meet my wants and needs?"

"Do I deny responsibility for problems in a relationship and simply see others as objects to manipulate for my self-glorification?"

"Do I see others as opponents to defeat and belittle so I can be dominant?"

"Do I regularly cast blame on others while never considering my own role in causing problems?"

These are important questions because you're basically asking yourself, "Do I socially and emotionally molest others? Are my relationships mostly about me?" If you're honest with yourself, you can greatly improve your self-understanding, your coping skills, and the quality of your interactions by working to minimize yourself as the primary focus. In other words, some self-analysis, even if you don't like what you see, is well worth the effort. An honest analysis will help you modify your actions by removing yourself as the primary element in your relationships.

Be aware, however, that there is a danger in such self-analysis. Looking inward can be an obstacle to effective coping if the process is not "reality-checked." That means you need a way to check if you are being objective. Without a reality check, you can easily develop some negative views of yourself:

Self-doubt: I don't have the courage and strength to change and recover.

Self-blame: I should have done things differently. This whole mess is my fault.

Self-pity: I have been victimized, and I deserve sympathy from others.

These self-intrusions make successful coping with stress almost impossible because you become unable to look objectively and accurately at the challenges facing you. One excellent way to resist these ventures into a self-centered mine field is to join a support group for those who have suffered the same or very similar trauma as you. Such groups are plentiful and can be located by contacting a local mental health association, crisis hotline, or even local law enforcement.

Support groups allow you to and realize it's not all about you. This is the golden rule of coping and is summed up nicely by a support-group member:

In my group, I discovered humility and caring . . . I mean to the point that I realized it was not all about me. I found out we all asked the same questions, faced the same demons, and needed lifelines. Since joining my group, I don't feel alone anymore and feel more human than ever before in my life.

And that brings us to empathy!

CHAPTER 5

EMPATHY

In our book *Using Psychology to Cope with Everyday Stress*, we said,

> Empathy. We usually think of it in terms of helping others, but it's more. If you have been previously victimized or are presently dealing with emotional upheaval in similar ways as another, who can understand their plight more than you? The true human beauty of empathy, however, is that both the giver (you) and the taker (the other) reap the psychological benefits. There is no more effective therapy than empathetic service to others. Whatever your plight, you are not alone in your difficulties. The best way to facilitate your ability to cope is to make sure that, as you travel the road to finding personal satisfaction, you leave no one behind.

Some people, for any one of a variety of reasons, choose to avoid discomfort by not allowing themselves to feel empathy. Instead, they choose a path of less resistance and resort to blaming others, projecting negative qualities onto others, or pitying others as unworthy of empathy. No matter which of these inappropriate paths is chosen, doing so robs these people of experiencing and enjoying the rewards of a life that involves genuine communication with others.

EMPATHY IS NOT SYMPATHY

When you're stressed and upset, you struggle to find ways to deal with emotions like fear, anxiety, guilt, grief, jealousy, and others who seem to rob you of stability in your life. At this point in the coping process, you think it's all about you. Why not? You're the one who's suffering, right?

Unfortunately, this self-centered emphasis makes coping difficult. Why? Because once you put yourself front and center as the victim, self-pity is not far behind.

Consider this hypothetical case. Jasmine was sexually abused when she was seven years old. She was in the second grade, and she got out of school before either of her working parents got home. One of their neighbors had a daughter, Betsy, who was enrolled at the local community college. Most of her classes were at night, and she was more than willing to babysit Jasmine every afternoon.

Occasionally, Betsy brought her boyfriend along. Jasmine's parents had said it was OK to bring him now and then but not every day. One day, when the boyfriend was along, Jasmine's mother called her and said she needed the car. Normally, Betsy walked to Jasmine's house, but that day she and her boyfriend needed the car to run an errand before going to Jasmine's house.

Betsy asked her boyfriend to watch Jasmine while she took the car to her house and then walked back. While she was gone, her boyfriend molested Jasmine with inappropriate touching and fondling. Twenty years later, we can imagine Jasmine describing things this way:

> I was absolutely horrified . . . terrified . . . scared to death. I knew what was going on was wrong, but I was

paralyzed with fear. I never told a soul about it. I felt too guilty, too ashamed . . . dirty, in fact. The best I could do was kind of push the whole thing to back area of my mind. I never forgot it, but it was there. If I ever dwelled on it, I knew all that shame and guilt and fear would come pouring out.

It wasn't until twenty years later that I told my story—to my support group of all things. As I got older there was one thing about me that was constant: I couldn't maintain any sort of a healthy relationship with a guy. All through high school, college, and afterward, I always found a way to destroy my relationships.

Finally, after a guy said to me, "You're an absolute sicko, Jasmine. You need help, or you're going to grow old alone. Get some counseling, will you?"

Turns out, I was talking with this one girl at work about it, and she said, "He's right. I'm actually in a support group for women who were sexually abused, and it's really helping me." And right then and there, that coworker was the first person I told about my experience that happened twenty years ago.

I ended up going to the group with her, and my life turned around. I learned so much about my guilt and shame and anger, but the main thing I learned was that I was feeling sorry for myself. I was abused . . . treat me gently . . . I deserve to be sheltered, protected, shielded from the realities of living. Not! The other girls got me off my pity train and taught me that just because I was abused, I had no right to expect someone to round off the corners of my world. Playing the victim just kept all those other negative emotions rolling around inside me, and the group showed me that I had to stop all the self-pity.

Jasmine's support group is an example of what most people think about when they think of empathy—that is, the group members can help Jasmine because they had traveled the same road. They knew and understood the emotional turmoil she was experiencing; that understanding allowed them to "reach" Jasmine because, in her mind at least, they had credibility with her.

When you get outside of yourself, face your troubles directly, and bring others who understand into the picture, your coping picture brightens. Whether you reach out to others with problems similar to yours, or work at trying to understand the effect you are having on others, substituting an "other-oriented," rather than "self-oriented," focus will provide insight into your problem. This other-oriented focus is what we mean by empathy.

When most people think of empathy, they also think of sympathy. If you can understand how another person is feeling, you are more likely to feel sympathy toward them, and this feeling motivates you to help them. Maybe so, but in a coping context, empathy has a much broader meaning than feeling sorry for someone. When you use empathy to cope, you are acting with *moral intelligence* (see chapter 3). You are using your own difficulties to reach out to another afflicted with similar difficulties.

> *The members of Jasmine's group don't feel sympathy for her; they identify with her. That identification allows them to relate to her in a mutually-beneficial give-and-take relationship that allows both parties to profit.*

There is, however, another role that empathy plays in the coping process. This role is quite different and more subtle than what we saw with Jasmine, but it still contributes to one's coping efforts. To illustrate this role, we'll consider the case of Irene.

Irene, seventeen, is being bullied by a peer, Lola, in high school. She does all she can to avoid Lola and stay out of the way of her wrath.

Problem is avoidance strategies don't work because they're a form of denial. Successful coping requires acceptance of challenges facing you.

Irene talks to her folks and other adults about the situation and begins to form some possible explanations for the bullying. Irene asks around, seeing if she can get a feel for Lola's family life, grades, anything that will help Irene figure out what Lola's angry about and why she's displacing that anger onto her.

What's Irene up to? Think about it. She's trying to get inside Lola's head to figure out why she chooses to bully her. Seems like a pretty sophisticated strategy for a seventeen-year-old, right? Of course, but it's a good one and one that illustrates the true dynamics of empathy.

So the bully comes up to Irene, pushes her, and says, "Look, b***h, get out of my way, or I'll beat the s**t out of you!"

Irene responds, assertively, "Back off, Lola. I get it that you're angry at something or someone, but you have no right to take it out on me. Keep it up, and I'll file a complaint with the school, and I'll win, and you'll get suspended. But I'd rather talk about it and find how you can point your anger at who deserves it. But not at me. No more!"

All of Irene's actions can also be included in what we mean by empathy. Irene's not looking to feel pity for Lola; she's looking to understand her so she can *stand up to her in the context of Lola's issues, not in the context of her fear of Lola.* Do you get it? Effective coping requires you to focus your actions on your values and your conscience and to convey your moral principles to your oppressor.

The absence of empathy is denial. Empathy can be used to generate acceptance of what is going on and assertiveness about what you can do about it. Irene can give the bully a choice because she has made hers. She uses empathy to produce acceptance, understanding, and a plan of action. Sympathy has nothing to do with it.

Jared and his wife, Helene, have a thirteen-year-old daughter, Karen. They both work, but Jared's schedule allows him to be home by 3:00 p.m., when Karen gets home from school. One day Jared is in the kitchen, and he hears a loud bang against the front door and some screaming. He runs to the door, opens it, and discovers another girl hitting his daughter right on their front porch. When the attacker sees Jared, she takes off running.

"What's that all about?" he asks his daughter.

"She bothers me every day on the bus. Today I pushed her, and she chased me all the way from the bus stop to home. I hate her."

Karen gives her dad the girl's name and says she lives on Harris Street. Jared gets out the phone book and finds the last name living on that street. With considerable trepidation, he dials the number. His heart is pounding because he knows confrontations with another parent can be a minefield.

"Hello," a woman answers.

"Is this Cindy's mother?"

"Yes, it is."

"This is Jared, over on Franklin street. My daughter, Karen, goes to school with Cindy, and they ride the bus together. Today Cindy chased my daughter from the bus stop to our house and was attacking her on our porch!"

"Well, Karen just told me that your daughter said that I was a whore!"

Jared's heart rate quickened even more as he sensed an impending explosion of rage from the mother. Could he manage to defuse the situation while being firm about the episode?

"Well, ma'am, I apologize for that, and I assure you I will have a talk with Karen, and she will not be saying anything like that in the future. I'm sorry. *But* I can't have your daughter attacking Karen. That's not right."

There was a pause, maybe five seconds, that seemed like an eternity to Jared.

"You're right. We can't allow that sort of behavior, and my husband and I will have a strong talk with our daughter." Another pause, allowing Jared a chance to collect his thoughts, but before he could speak, the mother continued. "You know, last year, I wish I had done what you just did."

"Ma'am? I don't understand."

"Last year my daughter was being bullied by a girl on the bus. It got so bad we finally had to go the principal's office and lodge a complaint. That caused a lot of hostility between the other parents and us. I wish I had just called the girl's mother and worked things out like adults."

A number of things are going on here. First of all, Cindy is an abused, bullied child who, one year later, becomes a bully. Her anger toward her abuser was obviously never resolved. Second, Cindy's mother experienced empathy toward Jared. She had been down this same road, and thanks to Jared's strategy of staying calm, polite, and reasonable, but assertive, the episode was settled amicably and maturely. There was no sympathy, no rage, no hostility, no threats. There was empathy, and it fostered a peaceful settlement of a potentially explosive issue.

At the outset of WW2, as Hitler began to unleash his war machine in Europe, England's Prime Minister Churchill argued with his senior government advisors about strategy: conciliation or prepare for war. Churchill had already shown empathy toward Hitler—that is, observed and analyzed him to understand him. He decided the German leader was a power-hungry sadist who would stop at nothing to attain world domination, and Great Britain had no choice but to prepare its defenses from an inevitable attack by Hitler. Churchill felt no sympathy for Hitler; instead, his empathetic analysis showed him that Hitler must be exterminated. Empathy—not sympathy, not hatred, not anger—allowed Churchill to prepare his country.

YOUR INTERNAL COMPASS

There's no secret to increasing your chances of being emotionally healthy and feeling good. These states *emerge* from your perceptions and interpretations about events and people around you and the actions you engage in because of those perceptions and interpretations. Emotional health evolves from a way of seeing the world and a lifestyle that gives you a sense of coherence, purpose, and the confidence to meet the challenges of life.

In a very real sense, if effective coping is a work of art, you are the painter, the creator of your personal masterpiece. For some people, their "work of art" emerges from religious faith. For others, it comes from a general spirituality about existence—something greater than themselves. For still others, it evolves from service to others, from experiencing the richness of the human enterprise. And this is just a small sampling of perceptions and actions that bring people good coping "artwork."

Whatever the source of effective coping, all of them provide an internal ethical and moral compass, a guidance system that directs actions that bring the actors—"painters," if you will—intrinsic satisfaction. This fulfillment is not dependent on material rewards or recognition from others; it exists in the good works carried out.

"Wow," you say, "I like that! Tell me how to create my masterpiece of living."

Sorry, no one can tell you how to go about finding your guidance system because, like happiness, it is not out there to be "found." Intrinsic guidance develops from honor, from the expression of social values, ethics, civility, and respect for others. It develops from exercising a social conscience. It's not something you can search for like circling a date on a calendar with the notation, "Beginning on this date, I am going to be happy, productive, and fulfilled!" Don't waste your time.

Do you need an expert to tell you what to believe? Do you need artificial chemical crutches to function? Faced with challenges, do you find yourself feeling passive, helpless, and needing someone to guide you? Your only escape from those "traps" is a moral compass, the key that unlocks your honorable self.

Many people who are suffering from stress, whether from a severe trauma or from an everyday irritant, do not realize that to cope with the stress, they must focus on their own *character*: their *ethics*, their *values*, their *integrity*, their *conscience*—all those traits that bring them honor.

These traits are also the seeds of humility and empathy,
and without the sprouts from those seeds, effective coping
will always be incomplete.

Dr. Carlea Dries, a former student, told me [CB] a story I share often because it is the best expression of empathy I have ever seen:

> Decades after his active-duty service during the Vietnam War, I asked a veteran how he continued to cope with the personal losses he suffered during the war and in the time since. He replied, "I celebrate their memories by fulfilling their bucket lists. I do what I can to continue their lives. I give hope for those who are lacking it. I don't attend pity parties. I read to those who lost sight because even though I lost things, I still can see. I get groceries for those who lost limbs. I do what good I can because there was a reason I was spared."

MESSAGES WITH EMPATHY

When you cultivate empathy from a base of honor, effective coping with everyday stress is greatly enhanced because understanding and appreciating the thoughts and emotions of others can provide you with personal insights. That's right! In a beautiful feedback loop, your moral compass helps build your honorable self, and that self, in turn, fosters humility and empathy, which strengthen your understanding of your honor.

Empathy also facilitates communication with others, and communication allows you to see that you are not alone—others deal with the same sorts of conflicts that you do. This sharing gives you a sense of humility that you are not the special one.

Finally, empathy helps you develop a giving/receiving interaction with others that brings everyone benefits. A giving/receiving interaction?

Think about that for a moment. Have you ever been hesitant to accept help from someone because you consider yourself independent and empowered? That's fine, but remember something very important: Independence and empowerment are strong signs of good coping, but when independence occurs without empathy, you risk social isolation; when empowerment occurs without empathy, you risk false pride.

When empathy is present, however, you are able to understand others' need to give, you become more willing to accept their help, and thus, you allow them to receive the special blessings of giving. What could be more satisfying and empowering?

Empathy can also help you in dealing with adversaries. Understanding why someone may want to be your opponent can give you insights and help you defuse conflict by showing others you understand their issues and insecurities. It's a tricky dance, but empathy can help show you the steps.

With all that in mind, let's talk about public social messages—words and phrases that are a part of our interactions with others. Psychologist Drew Weston has studied social messaging in a political context and how to design political ads with appeal to voters. This type of messaging can also involve what's called political correctness, an evil phrase to many people.

What we want to focus on, though, are words and phrases that fail to show an understanding of what another person is feeling. In other words, how can we interact with others and use our spoken words to better show our empathy? Let's consider some examples.

A former student once said to me [CB] that she worked with "food insecure" people. "I confess that I thought she dealt with eating disorders!" But no, food insecurity refers to those without regular access to enough food to provide for adequate daily nutrition. OK, that's fine, but could some people find the phrase "food insecure" vague and judgmental? Telling someone that they are insecure is not generally a compliment. On the other hand, what if the student had said, "I work with those without access to enough food to provide for adequate daily nutrition"? Would you agree this statement conveys more empathy than simply saying "food insecure"?

How about the phrase "unemployment compensation"? What sort of images do these words produce for many people? A lazy, no-good bum? A failure in life? Someone looking for a free handout? Someone so irresponsible that he or she can't maintain a job and gets fired a lot? These are not kind images.

But what if instead of "unemployment compensation," you said "financial support for people who have lost their jobs through no fault of their own"? This latter phrase is much more empathetic and results in a whole different class of images.

"Equal gender pay" is also one of those well-intentioned phrases that triggers all sorts of biases in some folks.

"Yeah, women can't do half the work of men, but they want the same pay anyway."

"Why should someone be entitled to pay they don't deserve just because they're a woman?"

"What about when they get all that time off for having a baby? Is that fair?"

On the other hand, instead of "equal gender pay," what if you hear "Everyone should receive pay that reflects their dependability, effort, productivity, and accountability"? Is that a little more empathetic and less likely to raise prejudicial thoughts?

We could come up with more examples, of course: Social Security, Meals on Wheels, immigrant dreamers, civil rights. But here's our point:

> *Others hear what we say with their brains, but they*
> *listen to us with their hearts.*

When you are able to reach your listeners' hearts, you are communicating with empathetic messages. And you know what will happen next? You will discover that your personal coping efforts will be greatly enhanced because you will realize you're communicating with *your own heart*. That self-discovery will bring you independence and empowerment with empathy. Your independence will be without isolation and loneliness; your empowerment will be without self-absorption.

Speaking to his brain, you say to your friend, Bill, "I hear you're having open-heart surgery next week. My dad had that a few years back, and he came through it great. You'll be fine, Bill."

Speaking to Bill's heart, you say, "I hear you're having open-heart surgery next week, Bill. My dad had that a few years back. I remember he said to me, 'Son, I'm scared out of my mind. I'm afraid I'll die on the table, and I'm not ready to go! I've still got a lot of living to do.' I remember his words so well, Bill, and they help me understand what you're going through. Any time you need to talk, I'm there."

Generally, when you think of coping with stress, we bet you tend to look for strategies that take place at an individual—me—level. When you throw humility and empathy into the picture, however, you transform your coping efforts into a social enterprise, and you experience the beauty of a life that includes others.

<> <> <>

GIVING ADVICE TO OTHERS

How do you handle things when someone reaches out to you for advice or just wants to get a sympathetic ear? Giving advice can be challenging because you are likely to be concerned about saying the wrong thing and making things worse. With that thought in mind, let's look at some general points when talking with others who are distressed:

As we just noticed above, there's a difference between "hearing" and "listening." This distinction is especially important when people ask for your advice. "Listen" to what others tell you; don't just "hear" them. Be uncritical to show them you understand what they are going through.

Show empathy: Remember, it's not about you but about them. "Here's what I would do if I were you" is not a helpful comment. You are not about "being them," so don't go there.

Demonstrate in your actions how important they are to you and what they mean to you. Offer to give them a ride, pick up their kids, stop by for a visit with some "food or goodies," etc.

Do not label them. ("Jane is bipolar, so I should offer to babysit her kids.") The labels will stereotype them in your mind and bias your interactions with them.

Use caution when discussing medications. You may feel that medications given for anxiety, depression, and other psychological issues only help reduce symptoms, but you should not force that view on others. If they are dissatisfied with their meds, encourage them to talk to their provider. Focus your talks on their life conflicts, not on their medications.

Help them keep their expectations realistic.

Here are a couple of hypothetical conversations that illustrate some basic principles to follow when talking with others. The idea here is not to memorize these examples and follow them to the letter; doing so would sound rather stiff and robotic. The point is to see the general strategies that psychologists have found to be effective when talking with others.

> *Comment:*   There's nothing for me to live for any longer. I don't care whether I live or die.
>
> *Response:*   All of us need to change our purposes and goals as life goes by. You had meaning in life before. I bet you can do it again and find some purpose in what you do. What do you think is holding you back?

Notice how the response does not criticize the commenter but suggests a proactive strategy and asks a question designed to distract the pessimist from self-destructive thoughts.

Comment: I've tried therapy, I've tried medication. None of it works. I might as well give up. My life isn't ever going to be worth anything again.

Response: Maybe you haven't had a counselor or medication that is effective for you. You haven't tried them all, right? Is there any harm in looking for a new counselor? Also, one thing for sure, people in counseling need to work at it to see positive change. Are you motivated to help yourself? Have you really given things a chance to work?

The response points out that the commenter has not exhausted his/her search. Also note how both replies serve to redirect the complainer from self-blame and self-pity and reexamine his/her efforts in a more realistic way.

One important thing to note about both these examples is how they rely on posing questions. If you're like most people, when you are talking to someone who is troubled, you will be tempted to express your opinions, forgetting that it's not about you but about the other person. Conversations with troubled folks will be much effective if you take yourself out of the equation and pose questions that encourage them to consider proactive *actions*.

Here are some more examples of conversations that illustrate some good ways to respond to troubled folks.

Comment: Life just sucks! It's just too hard. I'll never be the type who commits suicide, but I'll be damned . . . I don't care if I live another day.

Response: I agree life doesn't seem worth it at times. I imagine just about everyone has those feelings at one time or another. I've been

there too. But I bet most people would say
that life is what we make of it. Life deals
the hand, but we decide how we want
to play it. Have you asked yourself what
you're willing to face, what you need to do
to get more out of your life? Do you think
there are better choices you can make?

Note how this response centers on two things: empathy and
empowerment. The first part of the response says, "I hear you and
understand where you're coming from because I've been there." In the
face of total negativity about life, the second part focuses on optimistic
proactive coping strategies, using such phrases as "we decide," "what
you're willing to face," "need to do," and "better choices you can make."
The point is, rather than criticize the speaker, put the focus is on helping
them consider positive actions.

This next example deals with self-blame over past events:

Comment: I can't get over things that happened a
long time ago when I was a kid. These
memories haunt me. I'm damaged
forever. I can't overcome it. It's just no
use in trying. I've tried, but it's no use.

Response: I guess we all have our crosses to bear. Lots
of people have long-term problems dealing
with traumatic things. You hear about them
on the news all the time. But look at all the
stories of people who have moved on and
learned to cope with all kinds of traumas,
injuries, even death of a loved one. If they
can do it, why can't you? I bet a lot of them
got some counseling. Are you willing to
give counseling a try before you throw in
the towel? Isn't it at least an option?

This commenter is hung up on the past and determined to blame those who have damaged him/her. The response points out that many people must travel a rocky road of life, and the great majority of them have grown and prospered in spite of a lousy upbringing. Then once again, important questions are raised to help the commenter focus on positive actions that can be taken.

In these examples, note how both responses pose questions to the speaker.

> *Using questions tells listeners that confronting problems*
> *is up to them, and your questions imply you have*
> *confidence in their ability to do so.*

Comment: I don't know why I drink so much. Things go well for a while and then I do stupid things and just hurt myself with stupid actions. It seems like I go three steps forward and four steps back. What is my problem?

Response: I guess we don't always know why we do what we do. Isn't that natural though? But you're asking some pretty deep questions about why you're so self-defeating and self-destructive. Do you think a professional could help you find the answers?

Notice how the commenter is cleverly trying to trap the respondent into joining the pity parade. But the respondent doesn't fall for it and instead directs a question at the commenter forcing him/her to focus on the solution proposed. It's important to convey empathy to those who are troubled, but that doesn't mean joining their pity parade.

Comment: I don't know why I can't take my
medications and go to counseling like
I'm supposed to. Some days I don't want
to go to work or even get out of bed. Who
cares?

Response: Sounds logical to me. Why would you
care about taking your medicine or going
to doctors if you have this apathy about
life? Until you care, you're sure not going
to be doing much of anything that makes
you feel good. You'll just keep giving
yourself more pain. Is pain what you want
though? You have to decide because aren't
you the only one who can change your
life? Aren't you the only one who can
decide if you have a desire to live your
life to the fullest?

This response goes a long way toward expressing acceptance and understanding of the commenter. But a key question is also raised that challenges the commenter in a positive way: "Is pain what you want?" Again, notice how the response conveys empathy but goes on to challenge the listener.

To summarize, the main thing to remember when someone comes to you for advice and help is simple: It's not about you; it's about them. In these instances, we tend to say things like "You really shouldn't feel that way. You're being unrealistic. Plus, I have found that it helps a lot to . . . " Such comments, which substitute your perspective for the other person's, show a lack of empathy and understanding on your part.

*When talking to those who are troubled, resist the temptation to
express your opinion. Rather than tell them what to do, encourage
them to develop a feeling of empowerment by posing questions
to them to help them consider possible courses of action.*

Your job is not to tell them what you would do; your job is to encourage them to consider proactive options consistent with their needs and abilities.

<> <> <>

EMPATHY COMFORTS BOTH GIVER AND RECEIVER

Alan is a sixty-eight-year-old retiree. Eight months ago, his wife of forty-one years died after a brief illness. He still struggles with the loss, but he's getting along pretty well.

Victor lives in the same neighborhood as Alan. He's sixty-six, retired, and just two weeks ago, Benjamin, his partner for the past thirty-three years, died unexpectedly. Victor is devastated and fighting grief and loneliness.

Alan and Victor are casual acquaintances, although not friends. They recognize each other because they happen to take afternoon walks around the neighborhood at the same time each day. As they pass, they always exchange a brief greeting—"How's it going?"—and some small talk—"Cooled off nice since yesterday, didn't it?"

Thanks to the neighborhood grapevine, Victor learned about the death of Alan's wife and, shortly afterward, offered words of condolences on one of his walks. Through the same grapevine, Alan just learned about the death of Victor's partner and was hoping to see Victor resume his walks so he could express his sympathies.

Two weeks after Benjamin's death, Victor took an afternoon walk for the first time since his loss. As he and Alan approached each other, Alan thought, "My god, he looks awful. He's lost weight and is just shuffling along. He's really hurting."

When they got close, Alan stopped in front of Victor and said, "Victor, I heard the terrible news about Benjamin. I am so sorry. Please accept my condolences. How long were you together?"

"Thanks. I appreciate that. We were together thirty-three years," he replied as his eyes began to well up with tears while he stared at the ground.

"Oh man," said Alan, "I'm so sorry. I know the pain you're feeling."

"No, you can't know it," said Victor, still looking down. Victor's grief and self-pity just didn't allow him to accept this gesture of empathy from Alan. "You and me, we're different. We're from different worlds. You can't understand what Ben, a man, meant to me."

But Alan did understand; he knew how Victor was suffering, and he struggled to reply without offending him or adding to his hurt.

"How can you say that, Victor? We both lost our life partner, our rock, our friend who was with us for decades. And suddenly, they're gone. We just don't know how to fight the loneliness. I'm there too. I do understand."

Victor stood there looking at the ground and then said, "I guess you're right, Al. Maybe we have more in common than I thought. More than our differences. Thanks. Hearing what you said helps."

We believe that if this exchange actually happened, Alan and Victor would feel a jolt of self-actualization they had not experienced in a long time. Empathy does that. Learning that someone, especially someone who is superficially different, understands and feels your pain, that knowledge can be a powerful coping agent for both parties. Empathy plays a crucial and reciprocal role in coping with life's stresses. Alan and Victor would discover that and probably continue to exchange words on future walks. Might you also expect their words to go beyond casual greetings and end up helping each of them cope with their grief?

We see these principles during the 2020 pandemic. How many people object to wearing a mask in public, saying "It's my body, and I can do with it what I want. That's nobody else's business"?

These arguments miss what the mask is all about. The mask is about empathy—understanding and caring for others. When you're out in public and near others, every time you exhale, you could be threatening their health.

Returning to our Alan and Victor example, imagine if Alan says, "Here comes Victor. Too bad about his partner, but it was two guys living together. No way he is grieving and suffering the way I am." No doubt their conversation would be quite different from that described earlier. Sadly, stripped of empathy, both of them would miss out on experiencing a thick slice of humanity.

> *You want to cope with stress? Travel your road*
> *accompanied by empathy. If you lose it, you lose your*
> *humanity, and you will be very lonely and stressed.*

EMPATHY STRENGTHENS INDEPENDENCE

Independence is a good thing, right? When you're independent, you can stand on your own two feet, you can make decisions on your own, and you can forge your path with confidence. Best of all, you can do all this without being excessively dependent on someone else and allowing that person to shield you from the realities of life.

As we said earlier, however, the one thing you have to guard against is loneliness. Working hard to be self-sufficient can make you afraid to depend on someone. You can reach a point of believing that depending on others for any sort of help will make you appear weak and incompetent. So you avoid asking for or accepting help from others, and that can lead to social isolation. In other words, independence can be taken too far.

Mark is under a lot of stress at work. He's the chief supervisor of twenty-four workers who keep one section of an assembly line moving smoothly. He feels he must do everything himself, or he believes he's shirking his duties and his boss will demote him. There are many parts of Mark's job that can be delegated to his assistant, Lou, or sometimes even to one of the workers directly on the line, but he just can't do it.

Recently, Mark began experiencing increasingly bad pain in his knee. What was once a slight, almost unnoticeable limp developed into a very pronounced limp and an almost total inability to use stairs. Lou noticed his impairment and often offered to help in one way or another.

Comments like "Stay there and finish the paperwork, Mark. I'll go check the line," "Mark, let me give you a hand on the stairs," or "You better get that knee checked, Mark. I bet you need a replacement" often came his way, but Mark always misinterpreted the concerns as showing how much Lou wanted his job. It never occurred to him that these offers of help were out of genuine concern for his welfare.

Eventually, Mark became all but incapacitated and unable to do his job efficiently. His boss gave him an ultimatum: "Mark, get that knee fixed, or I'll have no choice but to let you go."

Mark knew he had to have the surgery. He was, however, plunged into anxiety about losing his job to that "backstabbing assistant of mine. That's the thanks I get for training him."

After surgery, Mark was homebound for several weeks. He became increasingly distraught and felt helpless about it all. He started to blame himself and was beginning to spiral into depression. During this rehab period, Lou visited him often and told him that things were going well at work and everyone was looking forward to his return. Mark could only think to himself, "Don't give me that bull s**t, you SOB. You're hoping I can never walk again so you can be the chief."

What's Mark's problem? Why does he see only threats coming from Lou? For a possible answer, let's consider the case of Franklin Delano Roosevelt (FDR), the thirty-second US president. After beginning what looked to be a great political career, FDR was stricken with polio at the age of thirty-nine and was never again able to walk without leg braces and assistance. Just standing, much less taking steps, was an immense undertaking involving considerable pain and effort, and he spent most of his days in a wheelchair.

Long before becoming president, FDR appeared to undergo a kind of psychological rebirth at a health spa in Warm Springs, Georgia. As the reality of his condition forced its way onto him, he became depressed and withdrew from society. Eventually, however, he found his way to Warm Springs after hearing reports that the waters of the spa had positive effects on paralyzed victims like himself.

FDR came from the "upper crust" of the American socioeconomic ladder, the elite of society. At Warm Springs, however, he interacted with, and probably identified with, everyday people he came to call polios. They were not the elite of society but victims like him. He interacted with his fellow polios as equals, without elitism, condescension, or superiority. In short, FDR discovered *humility* and *empathy*, which gave him renewed energy and drive. Within four years, he was governor of New York.

Returning to Mark, his interactions with Lou were lacking humility and empathy. Mark was the boss, and he felt that accepting help from Lou was beneath him and signaled weakness. Mark avoided facing this reality by convincing himself that Lou was after his job, and that justified his harsh feelings toward Lou.

Once Mark returned to work, still gimpy but improving each day, he continued to harbor suspicions about Lou. He began to watch Lou carefully and criticize him often. Lou became uneasy at this new and unusual treatment by his boss. As Mark became more and more critical of Lou, their relationship all but disintegrated, and Lou eventually left the company for another job.

Mark once again felt secure. The problem was he had never resolved his conflicted feelings and misinterpretations about Lou's behavior. It was only a matter of time before circumstances would arise that would reawaken these conflicts, and Mark would go through the entire mess again. And indeed, Mark's conflicts were reawakened when a new assistant, Martin, was hired.

Mark's interactions with Lou were fine until circumstances arose that Mark found threatening. Because humility and empathy were not a part of his relationship with Lou, the conflict would never be resolved. Without those crucial features of the relationship, Mark could hold on to his independence only by denying any signs of dependence on Lou. The result was loneliness, anger, and anxiety for Mark as he convinced himself that Lou was out to get his job.

Independence is good, but don't allow it to interfere with your relations with others who may truly have your welfare in mind.

Without humility and empathy, it will be difficult to recognize and reciprocate honorable, genuine intentions

of others. Your relationships will be in danger of
collapsing, and you will lose something worthwhile—a
sense of belonging.

<>   <>   <>

EMPATHY DEFICIENT

You might read these commentaries on empathy with a sense of frustration. Some people just have a great deal of trouble expressing empathy. Do you have a hard time feeling empathy for others when they suffer discomfort? If you do, you're not alone. It's kind of sad when you think about it. We are generally considered to be "social animals," but if you can't feel empathy for others, you really can't be fully "social." In that sense, empathy is probably one of the most honorable expressions we can give to others because it fulfills our destiny as social beings.

"Well," you ask, "if empathy is so crucial to being human, why do I have a hard time with it? I don't hate people. I like helping people, so what's my problem?"

Where might an empathy deficiency come from? The answer to that question can be complicated because it usually depends on the particular experiences and genetic makeup of each individual. Bill might be un-empathic for entirely different reasons than Sally.

Still, it is possible to come up with a general understanding of empathy deficiency if we think about empathy in a different way. That is, when you boil it down, *empathy means you are sensitive to emotional signals from others.*

Larry: Why do you think Roger is still suffering over Susan?

Declan: Didn't you see his face or hear his voice when you asked him how he's doing? Yeah, he said, "Just fine, the kids and I are moving forward, and we're doing OK," but that was bull.

It's three months since Susan died, but the guy is just eaten up inside. He's not coping well, and he needs support from a lot of people who have been down that road.

Declan seems to "get it," but Larry doesn't. Declan picked up on some cues that Larry didn't. So let's rephrase our question and ask, "How could a person develop an insensitivity to emotional social cues expressed by others?" Note how this question doesn't see an empathy deficiency as meaning someone mean-spirited, a misanthrope who generally dislikes people. That could be true for a particular individual, but looking at it as an insensitivity to social cues makes the deficiency more of a perceptual, not an emotional, problem.

Imagine being raised from birth in a home that is cold, rejecting, and full of criticism. Love and support are in short supply. In infancy, you learn that the world is not a trusting place; you can't depend on others to satisfy your needs, especially your need for comfort, warmth, soft cuddling, and gentleness. During your preschool years, the deprivation continues, and you are flooded with guilt ("What did I do wrong?"). You develop fear of showing any initiative or independent action; doing so will certainly result in abandonment by your parents.

As you grow older, you have no idea how to give and receive love. You have never been taught such interactions. Any developmental mirroring that occurred in your early experience was limited to frustration, uncertainty, and rejection. Furthermore, any thought of "giving yourself" to another in a context of love is threatening because it raises your core fear of abandonment. Love becomes threatening because it raises the risk of rejection.

Empathy itself is a threat to your stability. If you try to understand how others are feeling, you expose yourself to that situation in which you have no idea how to behave. Even everyday emotional social cues, like a smile or a laugh, a grimace or crying, become aversive to you. You learn to ignore them because they upset you, and you don't know how to respond to them.

If someone says with a smile, "You know, I really like you," you are threatened because you don't know what to say. Your cold upbringing did not prepare you for mutual caring and empathy. If a friend says, "I'm hurting ever since Gail dumped me," you're at a loss as to how to answer, how to offer solace, how to empathize.

You are frustrated and lash out at others, the only action you have experienced in your upbringing. Social signals, whether positive like a smile or negative like a frown, make you angry and foster conflict in your relationships with others, so you tune them out.

Are you doomed for life? No. People and events in your past helped make you who you are, but you are seldom perpetually enslaved by your past.

If your history of difficulty in assessing social signals is long enough, however, if it persists well into adulthood, you may need professional psychological help to unravel the various threads. Just remember, there's no shame in seeking help. It's the honorable thing to do, and in fact, you empower yourself by doing so. On the other hand, if you spend today blaming yesterday for your troubles, you will be unable to cope with the challenges of tomorrow.

The bottom line? You can learn empathy. With help, you can teach yourself to be sensitive to social cues. You can become a more active participant in the social enterprise of being human.

<>   <>   <>

ME! ARE YOU THE MAIN COURSE?

There is a long tradition in psychology that stresses people's need for meaning and purpose in their lives. From Maslow's thinking in the 1940s about self-actualization to present-day theories on mindfulness, psychology has always recognized the need for people to find ways to "be all I can be."

We believe that empathy and service to others plays an important role in this psychological growth. Talk to young people who are searching for who they are and what is their place in the world. Invariably, those who feel they are moving in the right direction are those who are involved in service activities. Time and again, we have seen college students resolve many of their conflicts and come to grips with the reality of their emotions, like anxiety, jealousy, and anger, by getting "outside" of themselves and giving to others.

On the other hand, those who believe they are the sharpest knife in the drawer, that the world somehow owes them something, these are the kids we find to have adjustment problems, deficient in relating positively to others, and who are frustrated and unprepared to discover that their opinions are not the most special or most accurate. These are the kids who lack humility and have an attitude of entitlement that brings them a lot of disappointment. Reality can be a harsh teacher, and when these kids don't get the special treatment they feel they deserve, they withdraw into a cocoon of avoidance and suffer significant coping problems as a result. Remember, withdrawal encourages self-criticism, which fosters feeling unworthy, which leads to feeling helpless, which makes you vulnerable to depression.

Me, me, me. I, I, I. When you lack humility, you form your own pity parade when things don't go your way. You wail about the unfairness of it all—"I deserve better!" You talk and think your way into becoming an emotional cripple. Humility helps you admit that you should not be the primary factor in the equation. There are always others involved. This acceptance can help release you from your personal pity parade, give you a sense of freedom that is uplifting, and instill in you an optimistic spirit. Strengthened with your newfound positivity, you will be more likely to "share yourself" with others who are also fighting stress in their lives, and here is where empathy enters the picture.

Empathy allows you to understand others in the context of their needs, not yours. That understanding allows you to focus your actions around human values and social conscience and to act in the service of moral principles. As we said earlier, what's nice about empathy is that both giver and taker benefit. Both of you discover that you are not alone.

<>   <>   <>

LESSONS FROM THE BUSINESS WORLD

Karen Gathercole is associate vice president of human resources at Florida Institute of Technology. In a news column, she discussed the human side of good HR principles. Her examples are all in a business-world context, but we think her comments reflect principles of effective coping.

Gathercole notes how any successful business boils down to its people, the human capital of the business. Employers should always make a concerted effort to understand the personality dynamics of their workers and how that personality is expressed in preferences for work conditions. An effective employer will investigate under what conditions individual employees are most efficient and, within reason, will strive to match those conditions to individual workers. When conducted at an individual level, this analysis looks at policies like work schedules, variations in work environment, child care, exercise opportunities, and even considers providing for diet preferences. Obviously, such investigation requires clear and respectful communication between worker and employer.

Gathercole also notes how communication is especially important in increasing productivity, maintaining employee morale, and giving workers a sense of company identity. Managing, brainstorming, building teams, fostering cooperation and compromise—these are all important contributions to the company "bottom line" without making workers feel like forgotten cogs in a wheel.

The best communication is face-to-face. The ease and convenience of our digital world often makes e-mails and texts relatively impersonal. These convenient forms of communication can fail to convey nuance in conversation and produce misunderstandings, frustration, and resentment. On the other hand, the clarity of body language, voice tone, facial expressions, and a host of other intangibles are generally enhanced in face-to-face interaction. Even phone interactions are usually superior to electronic messaging.

Following good HR principles will increase the likelihood of having workers who are satisfied with their employment, believe they are valued and appreciated, are willing to risk thinking "outside the box," and who feel somewhat empowered to play a role in policies.

A careful evaluation of these HR principles by reading "between the lines" should show you that they are also effective coping lessons for challenging conflicts and emotional upheaval in your own life.

Consider communication; how do you communicate with others? In conversations with others, do you impose your will on them and act like a dictatorial boss, always conveying the message that you know more and are in charge? Do you truly listen, or do you wait impatiently and interrupt to inject your opinion? Do you fail to put yourself in others' shoes and try to see things from their perspective? Do you use "I" frequently?

Clear, respectful, and genuine two-way communication is usually involved in effective coping and productive interactions with others. We repeatedly talk about the importance of communication with others in coping with the challenges of everyday life. You need to train yourself to monitor your reactions and comments when talking with others. You must work at understanding their perspective and recognize that although it may be different from yours, that does not make their perspective less valid than yours. You must realize that good communication works to find a middle ground between differing perspectives, not trigger an argument over whose perspective is better. You must treat others with courtesy, respect, and empathy. You must treat them as you want them to treat you.

Communication with others can be one of the best ways to cope effectively with life's curve balls because so often those curve balls come at you because of conflict with others. Seek out face-to-face interactions, and remember the four Cs of effective social communication: consultation, clarity, cooperation, compromise.

IS YOUR "DAILY LEGACY" HONORABLE?

How do you want to be remembered? What legacy do you want to leave behind? We're not talking about when you die. Sure, that's a part of your legacy, but we're asking how you want people to remember you at the end of the day. What do you want to be your daily legacy?

If you want to get along with people—and that means communicate better with them, understand their perspective when it's different from yours, and respect them as human beings—remember one simple thing: *People will remember how you make them feel.*

When you talk with someone about some disagreement, do you spend most of your time trying to convince them that your position is better than theirs? When the other person tries to do the same thing, the result will likely lead to dissatisfaction all around.

Imagine Betty and Frank arguing about some social issue. After going back and forth for a while, Frank says, "I just can't understand how you can believe that. You haven't done your homework. You're obviously biased and reached an opinion without giving it much thought."

If you were Betty, how would you feel? You've not only been insulted for holding an opinion that Frank considers wrong, but you have also experienced condescension and arrogance. Would you be irritated and angry at Frank? Would you be inclined to walk away and avoid any future conversations with Frank?

But what if Frank injected a little *empathy* into the situation? What if he gave in a bit and tried to see if there's a middle ground where you both can meet?

For example, suppose Frank says, "I understand your argument and can see where you're coming from. I get it, but I'm looking at the issue from a different perspective, and that's part of the reason for our disagreement. I bet if we talk about this some more, we might even come to some sort of middle ground. For now, let's just agree to disagree."

The thing about this comment is that it probably makes Betty feel worthy of the discussion because it gives validity to her position. She has been granted some credibility and will no doubt be willing to continue the conversation later.

The coping lesson here is that when you focus on how your words make others feel and not on trying to convince them that you are correct, social interaction can proceed much more productively.

Not only that, but others are also more likely to engage you in spirited conversation in the future. Wouldn't that bring you a sense of satisfaction and empowerment?

CHAPTER 6

PLANNING

COPING IN A PANDEMIC

The coronavirus pandemic of 2020 created coping challenges for people around the world. When you think about it, however, the pandemic provided all the elements of stress that you face on a daily basis: People felt a complete lack of control of events going around them. There was little predictability of what would happen next week, much less next month. There was concern not only for oneself, but also for loved ones who may become infected. People worried about their kids' education and future. As the pandemic continued, more and more people felt frustrated and lonely from social isolation, physical distancing, and wearing a face covering.

And then, as always, there were the media reports that described increased cases of people suffering emotional problems from it all: Reports said more and more people were seeking professional psychological help. Research was beginning to document all sorts of mental health problems—depression, anxiety disorders, outbursts of anger, guilt, insomnia—as a result of restrictions imposed by the pandemic. Even the dreaded PTSD was rearing its ugly head.

There's a special coping danger when it comes to media messages. Whether we're talking about a pandemic or any other social event, when you're surrounded by media messages and reports, you are at risk of "buying into them." In the case of the pandemic, reading about increased emotional problems can cause you to begin assuming that it's inevitable you will be victimized by those problems. You become caught in a self-fulfilling prophesy: (1) the pandemic is increasing mental health problems, (2) you decide "I'm under a lot of stress, and I'm going to develop an emotional problem," (3) you develop such a problem.

Consider the following exchange:

Interviewer: Why are you so stressed?

You: I'm worried that since suffering that stressful event, I'm going to develop PTSD.

What could be worse than developing a stress disorder because you're worried about developing a stress disorder? You have set the stage for a self-fulfilling prophesy.

"Does all this mean I am doomed?" you ask. Certainly not! Yes, the pandemic poses coping challenges for you, but so does a lot of what life throws at you. Consider things like loss of a loved one, divorce, unemployment, overdue bills, foreclosure, etc. All pose incredible coping challenges. So instead of folding up and withdrawing, what do you do?

You've read the answer many times in this book: *Accept* the reality of your situation; no denials using hoaxes, conspiracy theories, or other distractions. Be *accountable* for how you deal with your reality; no blaming someone else for what's going on. If today you blame others for yesterday's problems, you will be ill-prepared to cope with tomorrow's challenges. Find *humility* to admit that you're hurting and you may need some help. Reach out to others in a spirit of *empathy*; share your concerns with others and discover that you're not alone. Finally, develop a *plan* that allows you to cope with honor and reinforce your values.

Let's consider a plan for dealing with a pandemic. As we do so, take note of how the plan not only makes use of general coping principles we have covered, but also how the plan has components tailored to the specific demands of a pandemic.

First of all, make sure your plan encourages you to take actions that provide you with social connections. One of the hardest things about a pandemic is the requirement to socially isolate: no parties, no dining out with friends, no group activities. Maintaining physical distance from others creates feelings of social isolation, and a few things are more threatening or disturbing to humans. After all, we are social animals.

With that thought in mind, your plan should include regular "contact" with friends and family through platforms like Zoom. These are far superior to the static contact of something like Facebook. There's nothing like real-time contact with another that allows you to see others' facial expressions while you hear their voices.

If your plan includes professional help—and it should if you're feeling out of control, profoundly depressed, or concerned about harming yourself—look into virtual psychotherapy. One such program can be found at LiveWell-Coaching.com—a counseling platform developed by psychologist Mike Ronsisvalle that allows you to interact with a real person to help you deal with your stress problems.

A good coping plan will also include strategies for getting involved in service projects that allow you to help others. Such involvement will show you that others suffer like you, that you are not alone, and that you have empowerment strengths you did not realize. Let those strengths emerge from your supportive actions in service to others.

Here's the bottom line about any challenging situation: You must call on all your resources and decide the event does not make you helpless. There will always be some things involved in a crisis that you can't control; there will be others, however, you can control. Grab on to the latter to meet challenges. If you succumb to helplessness, self-criticism will follow—"I'm too weak to deal with all this"—and you will decide you must rely on someone else to live your life for you.

You are not weak, you are not evil, you are not helpless
and dependent, and you are certainly not alone. Let life's

challenges awaken your honorable self and spur you into
productive action to take care of yourself and others.

VALUES-DEFICIENT ANXIETY

"If everything is so great, why am I still so stressed about things? Something seems to be missing." Have you ever heard someone make a comment like that? "Something is missing from my life."

When you feel this way, of course, developing a coping plan is really hard to do. Having a plan requires you to have your ducks lined up, so to speak. You're able to say, "OK, I have some insight into my issues and have identified some actions that should help me through this. All I have to do is organize my thinking about carrying out my plan."

With that nagging feeling that something is missing from your life, however, it's really tough to reach that stage. Consider this possibility, however:

Very often that something missing involves your values,
and failing to link your coping efforts to those values
produces that "something is missing" feeling.

Think about your planned actions. Are they tied to your moral compass, your standards, your integrity? Most people say social conscience, empathy, and honor are important to them, but they fail to link these things specifically to their coping actions. They don't realize it, but that linkage failure is what is missing in their lives. The result? Anxiety or, more specifically, what we call *values-deficient anxiety* (*VDA*).

Dr. Carlea Dries shared with us what she sees as some linkage failures: "You put off investigating diets (an action), even though you say, 'I care about my health' (your value). You put off spending more time with your family (an action), even though you say, 'I love and need my family' (your value). You put off taking a course at the local college (an action), even though you say, 'I want to become more educated' (your value)."

Whenever you find yourself worried and anxious, consider the possibility that you may be experiencing VDA. To confront this type of anxiety, you need to examine your focus in life. For instance, do you focus on things you are *against*—a politician, a religion, an ethnicity, a nationality? If so, consider redirecting your focus from what you are *against* to what you *value*. Then you can work at coordinating your values with actions compatible with those values.

Actions are essential to effective coping, but those actions must be grounded in a "life strategy," which means your actions must serve your goals and ambitions in ways that complement your values. If you have not identified those values, your actions will not serve you in meaningful ways.

Think about it. If you believe you should instill personal accountability in your eighteen-year-old, yet you allow him to take his pet dog to college for emotional support, are you linking your values to your permission? If you believe in financial responsibility, yet tell your college-graduate daughter that being delinquent on repaying her college loan is OK, are you linking your values to your advice? If you believe you should be honest with friends but decide not to tell one of them you think she is being deceived by her romantic interest, are you linking your values to your silence? Unconsciously, such inconsistencies between values and actions can cause stress from VDA.

To cope with VDA, consider three questions: (1) "What am I avoiding?" (2) "Do I make life all about me?" (3) "Am I willing to develop a coping action plan that focuses less on me and more on the welfare of others?" The idea here is not to struggle with answers to the questions but to use the questions as paths to help you reflect on who you are and to develop actions that can help you move forward.

Instead of focusing on the anxiety you feel, reflect on those three questions honestly. This reflection will help you identify what is important to you and help you focus on actions dealing with those things. Remember, the idea is not to reflect on the anxiety you feel and how you wish you could get rid of it. How you feel is your reality, so don't work to deny that reality. The idea is to reflect on actions you can take to help you cope with your reality.

Many people get hung up on the third question. They have a hard time accepting that focusing on and empathizing with others is possible and will be productive. In short, they feel inadequate to the task. Keep in mind, however, that the idea is not to bring a special set of skills to the table; the idea is to base your coping actions on values that give you a social conscience—a respectful and sincere focus on others, not yourself. This focus will help you feel more confident and empowered to venture outside yourself and act independently.

"But these actions," you protest, "where would I even begin with things to consider?" Well, you might examine your feelings about various social issues: mental health; children's welfare; clean air and water; social, gender, and pay inequality; homelessness. No matter what the issue, finding an area that excites and involves you can bring you a wealth of satisfaction and redirect your VDA in a more productive direction.

Even when the source of your anxiety is clear, such as a pandemic like the coronavirus, VDA can add to your misery. How do you cope in troubled times? Do you sit at home feeling helpless? Are there people you value whom you could call (video or audio call, no text, no e-mail) and lend a reassuring voice and/or smile—human "contact"—for their comfort? Social isolation does not mean emotional isolation. Also, do you ask yourself, "Are there community support programs that fit my social conscience that I could support?"

During something like the coronavirus pandemic, to cope with the stress of staying at home and worrying of infection, in addition to maintaining your vigilance about handwashing and other protective measures, take time now and then to accept your anxiety as a normal reaction to reality and to reflect quietly on your values. Don't bother to write them down; let them emerge from positive introspection about who you are and the role you can play in the human enterprise.

Reflection on personal values is a type of mindfulness, the ability to be aware of who you are and what you're doing and how you can expand what you do for others. Your focus is not self-criticism or judgment. The focus is on finding ways to express yourself in ways that benefit others.

Here's the coping message: Whenever anxiety threatens to take hold of you, examine your values and then identify realistic actions you can take to complement those values. You will feel better—more confident, satisfied, and empowered to channel your anxiety into areas of your life in ways that give you some control over your actions. The case of Trisha shows precisely how this process can work and significantly help a coping plan.

<>   <>   <>

TRISHA CONFRONTS HERSELF

Trisha is twenty-seven years old, married, no children. Fifteen months ago, she suffered a miscarriage while pregnant for the first time. She was devastated as only women who have had a similar experience can understand. She was in counseling for a couple of months. The counselor recommended she supplement her sessions by joining a support group of women who also experienced miscarriage.

"The group will add a new dimension to your recovery plan," the counselor said, "and I think you'll profit a lot." And indeed, Trisha found that relating with other women who understood her pain brought her a lot of comfort. She did, however, have one concern.

"It's interesting," Trisha says, "I've been in the group for eleven months. The girls are great and give me a lot of support, but whenever I tell my story, like when a new member joins, I still break down and cry like it happened yesterday. It's been over a year, and I still get emotional."

Like most people who enter counseling or other types of support programs, Trisha expected positive results within a reasonable period. The problem is what is a "reasonable time" is not etched in stone. If Trisha's case were real, for instance, after more than a year in treatment, should she be able to relate her story without crying?

People undergoing counseling often ask, "What actions mean I'm not coping well with my trauma?" Is Trisha's crying, for instance, a sign of poor recovery? Should she be able to relate her story calmly and objectively to consider herself on the road to recovery?

So we have two issues occupying Trisha: the length of time she's been under treatment and her unexpected crying. Trisha must accept the fact that if she is progressing in coping with her trauma, the time frame is not really an issue. She needs to be able to say, "There will always be a part of me that shows a permanent scar. No matter how long it's been, I really can't expect it to disappear."

As for the crying, Trisha says, "I used to think all my crying meant that I'm a failure and not coping well. But the girls in the group helped me see that I'm basically an emotional type. I mean, growing up, I was always one of those 'Omigod! Omigod!' types who made everything a catastrophe. That's who I am. If I start crying, I'm just being me."

Trisha must learn that she is linking her crying to her recovery, and that is inappropriate. She is focusing on her emotions, a natural part of who she is, instead of focusing on her thinking. As we noted in chapter 2, criticizing yourself for your emotions is denying a part of yourself.

Evaluating her coping plan requires Trisha to focus on her thinking and reframe how she thinks about herself and her crying. She needs to understand that she is an emotional person and may begin crying whenever she talks about her experience But that's OK as long as she understands and accepts the pain she is feeling. Her focus must be on that understanding, not on how she expresses her pain. She must realize that crying doesn't mean she should feel guilty or believe that what happened is her fault.

<> <> <>

RESOLVING A CONFLICT AT WORK

Sharon enjoys her job, except for one thing: She finds one of her colleagues, Eric, a royal pain. He thinks he's hot stuff, and when around

Sharon, he acts arrogant and likes to make flirtatious comments directed at her.

Showing some empathy, Sharon says, "He doesn't mean any harm, but he's one of those guys in his early thirties who acts like he's still a college frat boy. He never really grew up. So he often makes these not-so-subtle sexist comments directed at me or says how attractive something I'm wearing is. No touching, no hostility, just being a pain in my butt. I tell him to grow up, but he usually just laughs. He acts like a teenage kid teasing his sister. Like I said, harmless, but I'm getting tired of it, and I need to deal with him without poisoning the work atmosphere." Those last words, "without poisoning the work atmosphere," are worth remembering because they show one of Sharon's values about her job: It's important to foster a positive work atmosphere.

In developing a plan to deal with Eric, we know Sharon needs to focus on five other coping areas:

Acceptance. Eric is a problem, and he's not going away without intervention. His behavior irritates her, that's another reality, and she must not try to make herself feel less irritated. That sort of denial would have her turn a problem-based conflict into an emotion-based one, and she will fail.

Accountability. Sharon must make Eric accountable for his behavior and force him to face consequences. By the same token, Sharon must accept responsibility for resolving the situation because Eric will not.

Humility. Sharon must admit that she is no more valuable to the company than is Eric. She need not complain or whine to others as if she deserves special consideration.

Empathy. She needs to understand Eric's perspective. She's already there, actually, because she describes him as a young man still fixated on childish college fraternity-type behavior.

Values. Sharon needs to ask herself, "What do I value about my work and my employer? How does Eric's behavior threaten those values?"

Sharon thought through her *coping plan of action.* She had a private one-on-one meeting with Eric and told him his flirtatious, immature behavior had to stop—she made him *accountable.* She showed him specific parts of the company employee handbook and pointed out that she had a basis for filing a complaint but didn't want to do so for the sake of office morale—one of her work *values*. She showed *humility*—she did not threaten to play a card based on her gender, but she did so with a dash of assertiveness, basically demanding he take responsibility for his actions.

Notice how Sharon did not decide to let things ride and avoid confronting Eric. She *accepted* the reality of his behavior, the emotions it generated in her, and the likelihood that it would persist. She also accepted that she had no control about what he might choose to do on a given day.

We already saw how Sharon was empathetic about Eric's immaturity, and that helped her stay calm—that is, she knew she had to confront him. She was able to do so from a task-based, not an emotion-based, context. She used the employee handbook, not an emotional outburst involving threats, to make her point.

Sharon clearly put the ball in Eric's court. His actions were up to him, but if he refused to see things from her point of view—notice how she required Eric to show *empathy* for her—there would be consequences. Once again, Sharon placed *accountability* squarely in Eric's lap.

Sharon enjoys her job and believes in integrity, reliability, teamwork, respect for her colleagues, and loyalty to her employer. Her workplace values are honorable. Her plan of action was guided by these *values* and allowed her to be open—not overreact—to her frustration and irritation caused by Eric's behavior and allowed her to confront—not avoid—the troublesome situation.

Finally, note how Sharon still has a card to play if necessary. If Eric does not change and treat her with more courtesy and respect, she can go to plan B—the employee handbook and file a formal complaint.

FIGHTING HELPLESSNESS

Laura is thirty years old and periodically physically abused by her husband. She never knows when she will be hit, slapped, pushed to the floor, or thrown against a wall. There are other times when her husband is affectionate, helpful, and caring. She sees her only hope as trying to stay at peace with her husband. "If I run, threats against my kids and other loved ones will be carried out. What about my financial future if I leave him? Keeping him calm is my only option."

A part of Laura's problem is that her husband's behavior is unpredictable. Sometimes she is rewarded with kindness and warmth, but at other times she is yelled at, threatened, or physically attacked. Psychologists know that such unpredictability can produce strong submissive behavior from victims. When you think about it, that makes sense: Victims become agreeable, polite, and solicitous toward "the enemy" in the hope of avoiding attacks. In short, they develop strong dependency actions in a desperate attempt to avoid harm.

We see this sort of behavior in many circumstances: the bullied kid on the playground tries to join his tormentor's group; a kidnap victim admires and identifies with her captor; an abused child affectionately rushes to her abusive daddy's side when he comes home from work; sex-trafficking victims make no effort to escape their "handler"; Laura displays the role of an adoring spouse.

Well-meaning friends and relatives who sensed Laura's problem asked, "Why don't you leave him?" Laura would like to end her marriage, but she says, "I have no job and nowhere to go. Even if I did, he'd find me and beat me. And I'll never go to the cops because he said he'd kill me. I'm just totally helpless."

> *"I feel totally helpless." This comment, while completely
> understandable, is a crucial warning signal. Helplessness
> will inevitably lead to self-criticism and self-blame, and
> depression will not be far behind.*

Reggie is sixty-eight and lives in low-income housing in an inner city. Drugs and gang activity are rampant in his apartment complex. His apartment has been burglarized a couple of times, and he has also been robbed once while walking on the street. Reggie lives in perpetual fear of being attacked or robbed and feels totally helpless. In fact, after one of the burglaries, the police captured the perpetrator. When asked if he was willing to testify against him, he said, "No. What's the use? He'll just get off and come after me. I got nothin' to fight him."

Like Laura, Reggie feels totally helpless.

Psychologist Martin Seligman developed the concept of learned helplessness to explain cases like Reggie's and Laura's and their complete inability to take control of their situations. The unpredictability and inescapable circumstances of their treatment has taught them that there is nothing they can do, so why bother to fight it? Why should Reggie bother to testify? The crook will come back madder than ever. Laura talks about divorce, but she may never be able to do so because of her feelings of helplessness. Both she and Reggie basically feel that they have lost control and have given up.

Not surprisingly, learned helplessness is a precursor to depression. Victims feel their lives are spinning out of control, and they have learned that it is all but futile to try and do something about it. The consequences are frustration, anxiety, and despair, followed by apathy, withdrawal, and finally depression. No matter how bad their lives become, no matter how bad the pain, they figure, "Why bother to fight it? There's nothing I can do about it."

> Our message is: You can do something about it; you can learn to take control of your lives to empower yourselves. You can accept the reality of your situation and resolve to change it, even if doing so means you must suffer further.

Unfortunately, once learned helplessness takes control, it is difficult to hear this optimistic empowering message and easier to give up. Sometimes you must take the rockier coping road.

What could Reggie do? A first step might be in trying to organize his neighbors into fighting the perpetrators who commit crimes against them. There is great strength in numbers. If they seek police advice on ways to form a neighbor protection group, and if they tap into legal resources available to low-income victims, they just might discover that following these strategies, over which they have control, might bring them significant positive results.

How about Laura? She could listen to her friends who continually argue that she needed to take action; they also said they would support her every step of the way. They gave Laura the confidence she needed.

Laura should contact a women's resource center and legal aid for advice on how to proceed. She might to a resource center facility that housed women like her. She could get a divorce attorney and involve the police by getting a PFA order. Her friends could help her fight her apathy and dependency. The best antidote to depression is action. Laura has many action options.

It is important to remember that just because you feel you have no direct control over the source of your troubles—and often you don't, be it a spouse, criminal, supervisor, or acquaintance—there are always options available to you that allow you to exercise control in other ways. That's where the coping plan comes in, a plan that includes those options, a plan that focuses on your problem, not on your emotions. A problem-based focus will give you specific aspects of situations to attack and help you make sure you have resources backing you up.

The one thing you must not do is move into apathy/surrender mode and make those actions your habitual response to your troubles. You must determine your "circle of control" and, operating within that circle, fight!

The important coping lesson here is that you must be on the alert for tendencies to learn to be helpless about things in your life. Being vigilant about feelings of helplessness and apathy will help you avoid a major danger: becoming overly dependent on someone. Helplessness makes you vulnerable to buying into those who preach the message "Only I can help you out of your desperation." If you fall for this message, you are in trouble because your excessive dependency will make independent action on your part all but impossible. Autonomous action on your part is essential to effective coping; unfortunately, excessive and inappropriate dependency on another will cause you to let the other person do everything for you, making you weaker than before.

Rather than reaching out to false messengers who do not have your best interests in mind, you must organize your coping efforts around your proactive plan of action. Obviously, like both Laura and Reggie, you can reach out to others for assistance but not to the point that you totally depend on them.

<> <> <>

IRRATIONAL THINKING

Coping with stress requires you to accept certain aspects of your life rather than try and manage it. Management is a form of denial. Think about it. Suppose you have kids who are very energetic and act out a lot. Someone tells you to "manage" them better. What do you think they mean by that? Finding places for them to act out or working to keep them quiet and out of the way? We bet it's the latter. Let's face it. To most people, managing kids means stifling their energy, even medicating them if need be, to avoid or at least minimize their disruptive influence.

It's the same with anger. When might someone say to an acquaintance, "You should take a course on anger management"? Probably right after the acquaintance has exploded in an outburst of anger. Managing anger means learning to suppress the anger, keeping it from exploding, getting rid of it. That's awfully close to denying it.

Manage your life? Most people are telling you to get rid of the "bad" parts and treat them as if they no longer exist. Problem is the "bad" will still exist, but you have no idea how to make them what they are—a part of you.

> *Effective coping requires you to work on your relationship with yourself—who you are, including the good and bad parts.*

So there you have it . . . back to acceptance of who you are and what's going on in your life. As we have said before, one of the first steps in coping is acceptance of yourself. Remember, acceptance doesn't mean you like everything about yourself; it simply means facing the reality of yourself.

A part of that reality is carrying irrational thoughts around, and successful coping requires you to challenge the negative and irrational thoughts that occupy you. Everyone has such thoughts now and then, but trouble begins if you have them most of the time. Here are some examples:

Making mountains out of molehills. Frank made a mistake at work and thought he was going to be fired. Not only was he not fired, but his "mistake" also uncovered a flaw in the company work manual.

Taking everything personally. Is the slightest criticism from others a challenge to your self-esteem? Remember, you can't control what others say. Marian felt that whenever her husband decided to do something with the guys, it meant he felt she was a lousy wife.

It's not a black-white world, so don't force others into one. "You either trust me or you don't." "I am always correct, and he is always wrong." This style of thinking overlooks a basic truth: There are two sides to every story, and the truth often lies somewhere in the middle!

Do you overgeneralize and reach crazy conclusions from a single unrelated incident? If so, you will be inundated with irrational thoughts that will shower you with feelings of unworthiness, shame, low self-esteem, and hopelessness.

"I gave a lousy presentation. I'm obviously a complete failure in everything I do."

"I got a lousy grade in my economics course. I may as well quit school."

"I was turned down for a date, so I'm obviously a worthless individual no one wants or cares about."

"I must succeed in everything I do, or I'm a failure."

"I must be admired and respected by everyone, or I'm worthless."

"I put some incorrect data in the work project. I'm a burden to the team."

"The boss said I need to work faster. She obviously thinks I'm incompetent."

You dishonor yourself when you engage in thoughts like these. You impair your day-to-day functioning as your life becomes organized around the central themes of those thoughts. The thoughts are demoralizing, interfering with effective coping, and making you vulnerable to psychological dysfunctions eventually. Your mind entertains a big package of irrational thoughts, and you are constantly adding thoughts to the box. The result is that you worry about a variety of different things and at an intensity far above what is normal concern and worry.

The repetition of irrational thoughts in your mind will dispose you to focus on them more and more. As you do so, your actions will be modified around those thoughts, and you will develop dangerous habits of withdrawal and denial. You know from reading this book that finding satisfying actions for yourself is central to effective coping. Actions that service irrational thoughts do not bring satisfaction because they are difficult to resolve and tend to isolate you from situations that need to be challenged.

Imagine this hypothetical situation: A woman in counseling confesses that she avoided social situations as much as possible because "I'm afraid I will faint." In the following exchange, note how the counselor works to challenge her irrational thinking.

> *Counselor:* Afraid you'll faint? Has that ever happened?
>
> *Woman:* No, but it's possible.
>
> *Counselor:* Yes, that's true. But can you accept that it's highly unlikely?
>
> *Woman:* Yeah, I can go with that.
>
> *Counselor:* Besides, what if you did faint? What's the big deal?
>
> *Woman:* People would laugh at me and think I was worthless.

Counselor: Worthless? Laugh at you? Would you react that way if you saw someone faint?

Woman: No, I would think they were sick or needed help. I wouldn't . . . Oh, I see what you mean. No, all right, maybe they wouldn't make fun of me.

Here's a more detailed example of challenging irrational thinking. This case also involves anxiety about thinking, "What if I look like a fool? Everyone will probably think I'm mentally ill or something." The irrational thinking of being labeled mentally ill is not at all uncommon and can easily lead you down a self-defeating path of avoidance and poor coping.

Woman: I picture myself walking in a crowded mall and getting so panicky that I faint.

Counselor: You faint? Has that ever happened?

Woman: No . . . but it could.

Counselor: I don't think it's likely that you will faint if you engage in some of your relaxation breathing exercises. But what if you did faint? Why would that be so bad?

Woman: Are you kidding? I would look like a fool. People would think I was an idiot . . . a total ass, maybe even mentally ill.

Counselor: If you were walking in the mall and saw someone collapse, would you think they were some incompetent loser or mentally ill?

Woman: Hmmm. Well . . . I don't know . . . I guess not really when you think about it . . . I guess I would think they were sick or something . . . maybe hadn't eaten or taking some medication. No, I guess . . . no, I wouldn't think they were a loser. Probably had some physical problem.

Counselor: So what does that tell you about how realistic your fears are? And by the way, suppose you really do faint. You wake up, and people are standing around you, laughing, pointing at you, and saying, "What a loser! Can't even shop in the mall!" Someone else says you must be a mental patient.

Woman: My god, I would die of humiliation?

Counselor: You would physically wither up and die?

Woman: Well . . . I would at least be embarrassed as hell.

Counselor: Well, good luck going through life without being embarrassed at times. But remember, you can't control how others react. You can, however, control how you evaluate situations. You can enable yourself to say, "So what if I faint? If someone sees me as a loser, that's their problem. The fact is, plenty of people around will help me and I'll get through it."

"OK," you ask, "how do I deal with irrational thoughts?" One thing for sure, simply telling yourself, "I've got to stop thinking this way" is futile. Your best bet is to *accept* the reality of your irrational thinking, *identify* the thoughts, and focus on rational *actions* you can take that will help you think more realistically.

Look again at our earlier examples. Instead of carrying around that irrational baggage, how about considering strategies that involve more proactive self-talk.

Gave a lousy presentation? "I need to prepare better for the next one. I'll ask Joe for some suggestions."

Got a lousy grade? "I need to find a study group, plus talk to the prof for suggestions."

Turned down for the date? "Fred says I scared the girl by suggesting she come to my place for dinner for our first date. I better change my approach to asking a girl out."

Must always succeed? "I need to analyze my failures so I can improve next time."

Think about it. When you react to failure by developing proactive actions to try to improve, you are learning how to fail, and that's a good thing.

Many people are crushed by failure and unable to cope with the resulting anxiety, frustration, and other disheartening emotions. When you learn how to fail, however, you see failure as an opportunity to improve, and you accept the challenges imposed by failure. Then you are coping effectively.

The first step in the process is to become aware of your irrational thoughts. Write them down when they occur. Enlist the help of friends, acquaintances, and even professionals to help you identify them. In this way, you will be able to focus more on rational courses of action to help you cope with the everyday challenges you face.

There's never any guarantee you will succeed. But by focusing on positive actions, at least you're teaching yourself to persevere even when frustrated, you're showing yourself that you are self-sufficient enough to engage in some proactive actions, and you're doing things that give you a chance to feel good about yourself. Such positive possibilities certainly outweigh marching in your personal pity parade.

Be realistic about the stress in your life. Are you ruled by irrational thoughts, such as "I must be perfect and succeed in everything I do, or I am a worthless person"? That thought dishonors you. A more realistic thought would be, "If I fail, I will examine what I did wrong and take steps to correct my mistake so I will be less likely to fail the next time." That's a reaction that involves honor.

When faced with the reality you failed, honorable
coping involves framing that failure as a challenging
opportunity to improve.

Is it really so hard to put things in a realistic perspective by balancing those events beyond your control with those you can control? If you're stressed about driving to a meeting across town, how difficult can it be to say, "I have no control over how bad the traffic will be, but I can leave early so heavy traffic will not make me late. I can also map out alternative routes in advance in case traffic backs up"?

When you are stressed and feeling overwhelmed, you have to guard against feeling sorry for yourself and asking others for sympathy. There are always alternative upbeat actions you can take. Instead of being dominated by irrational, self-serving thoughts, find those realistic actions that will serve you well.

<>   <>   <>

COLLEGE CLASS OF 2020

You're the oldest of generation Z, born between the mid-1990s and early 2010s, and you're a member of the college graduating class of 2020. You made it! You achieved your goal of earning your college degree. Time to head out into the real world and make your way, right? Except the coronavirus got in the way of your plans.

You didn't even get a commencement ceremony. The whole family was going to get together and celebrate with you. Bummer. But you can handle that. After all, a job application will ask if you have a college degree; the application will not ask if you had a graduation ceremony.

Still, the virus has thrown a lot more curveballs your way than just that ceremony. Maybe you had a summer internship lined up and felt pretty good it would lead to a job offer. It's been canceled. If you majored in a field like nursing or physician assistant, you're really in trouble. You needed to complete professional rotations over the summer before you could even receive your degree, but hospitals and medical centers have largely canceled positions for those rotations. You're on hold. The economy is shot, the number of job postings online is in the toilet, and you're living at home. You're broke and not even eligible for unemployment compensation.

You don't see a lot of options for yourself right now, do you? Rosy statements from the president—"We're back!"—don't do it for you, do they? Your self-esteem is ravaged. You're full of self-criticism and anger. Your personality feels robbed, empty, helpless, and worthless. You're spending too much time in that depressing wasteland called social media, trying to rally others to join your pity parade.

Sounds pretty bleak, especially if you believe that human beings are pretty weak when it comes to coping with grim reality. Well, shed that belief and get off the woe-is-me train. Humans are not weak; we are hardy or we wouldn't be here. A challenging environment would have extinguished us long ago.

Fact is humans have survived, so far, because we're sturdy, flexible, adaptive, tough, and durable. Those are honorable traits, and when you disown them in your life, you sacrifice your honor.

OK, so you didn't get your precious commencement ceremony. Will this be your future excuse when your coping efforts go down the tubes?

Accept it—it happened. Life is full of disappointments. Be accountable. Don't waste your time looking for someone to blame for your predicament. It's real and finding a scapegoat is not going to make it go away. Resolve to use your strengths—your intelligence, judgment, initiative, and social skills—to devise a plan to get you moving forward again. Be accountable to your strengths. And remember that your plan should include two crucial components that only you can provide: *humility*—it's not always about you—and *empathy*—you must be sensitive to the needs of others.

"Well that's just great," you're thinking, "but how am I supposed to do all this fancy-sounding stuff?"

Listen to what a couple of your Gen Z cohorts have to say about that. These comments come from an issue (June 1/8, 2020) of *Time* magazine.

Salvador Gomez-Colon is a teenager from Puerto Rico. Remember, just a few years back when Puerto Rico was virtually demolished by hurricanes Irma and Maria? Faced with a destroyed electric grid, Salvador came up with a simple goal: For Christmas, illuminate each home in Puerto Rico with solar lightbulbs. Go for it, Salvador! Today, faced with the challenges of coronavirus, Salvador is at it again and says, "There are countless ways to support each other even as we remain physically separate, whether it's sewing masks for vulnerable populations or writing thank-you notes to essential workers."

Then there's Abigail Harrison. Abby is twenty-three and came to national attention in 2010 when she said she wanted to be the first astronaut to walk on Mars. Reflecting on troubling times in 2020, she says, "I've seen people risk their lives to care for others. And most incredibly, I've seen masses of people choose to cast themselves into isolation to protect people they will never know." Abby sees the glass as half full and is one of those people who can squeeze the positive out of the most negative circumstances: "Losing so much control over our lives, combined with the isolation that comes from social distancing, has made the pandemic feel nearly impossible to overcome. Know what else feels nearly impossible? Going to Mars. But I assure you, they're both possible."

> *The key to coping with stress is to get into task-based mode—"I can contribute to this effort"—and get out of emotion-based mode—"This is not fair!"*

Whenever you have to cope with the challenges of your frustrating and depressing emotions, you must act with honor. You must get off your duff. What organizations in your area need volunteers? Contact them and offer your services. Or ask yourself how you and your friends might organize and offer services and materials to people in your community who are suffering. Feel the pain of others, reach out to them, offer your services.

There are also a number of service initiatives at a national level that offer opportunities to volunteer in areas like national parks, retirement homes, Habitat for Humanity, animal rescue, libraries, food pantries, Red Cross, and political campaigns. You may scoff at volunteer activities, but remember, they offer collateral opportunities for networking, expanding your knowledge and problem-solving skills, and discovering new career paths that fit with who you are.

When you get involved in service activities, you will experience satisfaction like you never have before. You will learn how working with others in a common venture will nurture your development of a social conscience. You will learn how to communicate with others—how both to speak and listen. You will learn humility and empathy and discover a two-way street where you receive even as you give. You will enjoy the beauty and grace of other people and see that there are fulfilling discoveries along a meaningful and enjoyable road of life. And when that first job comes along, you will be prepared to profit from it in ways you didn't expect.

DEPENDENCY AUDIT

You have a friend, Ron, and you think he's the greatest thing since sliced bread. He always seems to have the answer. He knows how to handle situations that make you feel uncomfortable; he knows how to handle people. You feel comfortable, secure, and safe when you're with him.

You hang around with Ron a lot, and he starts to "rub off" on you. When Ron laughs, you laugh. When he's angry, you get angry. When he explains something, you accept it as truth. When he tells you something is false, you believe him and discount it. You ignore criticism of Ron.

You may not realize it, but you have become inappropriately dependent on Ron. This is OK, of course, if you're three years old and Ron is your dad, but it's not so good if you're an adult. Such total dependency makes it impossible for you to evaluate and cope with reality in any objective way because you are compelled to see reality as your idol wants you to see it.

In a sense, you belong to the cult of Ron. He is your unquestioned leader, and you are his loyal follower no matter what. If you ask Ron about information that seems to contradict his teachings, Ron will explain why you must avoid false facts that only mislead and deceive you. Over time, again and again and again, Ron will remind you of the false messages and saturate you with his truths. This pure repetition will literally rewire your brain to accept what Ron says. If you deviate from his "correct path," he will distract you and substitute convenient scapegoats to correct your inappropriate thinking. You come to think like Ron, act like him, incorporate his standards into your thoughts and actions, and sacrifice your self-worth and self-respect.

In the context of coping with stress, such excessive dependency on another is incompatible with developing self-empowerment, critical thinking skills, and self-confidence. This extreme dependency prevents you from developing self-efficacy and being able to initiate independent action. You will not be in touch with *your* thoughts and *your* actions. You will likely blame other people or events for your current problems. Your optimism will not be grounded in reality but on your leader's version of reality. You will withdraw from stressful situations, waiting for your leader to handle things. In short, psychologically, you become a dependent, helpless child.

Do you want someone else to tell you how to think and act? Do you want someone else to tell you what is true and what is false? Are you so insecure that you need to cling to another out of fear of abandonment from a metaphorical parent? If you feel uneasy about your unquestioned allegiance to someone who dictates your life to you, then it is time for you to *audit your relationships* and check for excessive dependency that will rob you of personal autonomy and the ability to cope with everyday stress on your own.

What we're saying is if your coping plan is designed mostly by someone on whom you're excessively dependent, the plan won't work for you, and you will never find your honorable self.

<>   <>   <>

WHATABOUTISM

Every parent has heard it: You ask your nine-year-old son why he cheated on his test in school. His answer, "Well what about Johnny? He cheats all the time." What about . . . ? This desperate attempt to avoid accepting accountability is hardly limited to children. Few politicians can complete their tenure in office without pleading, "You criticize me for this action when it was shown again and again by my predecessor. What about her?"

Whataboutism is a close cousin of rationalization, and using it is probably one of the most dishonorable ego defenses available. You got caught, and you can't accept responsibility for your action. You screwed up big time, but to admit it would be a serious blow to your fragile ego. So you shout out, "I only did what everyone else does!"

When it comes to coping, whataboutism is just another one of those exercises in denial. How can you be to blame when everyone else does it? Your denial protects your ego, but it is damaged, weaker than before, and vulnerable to severe consequences next time. Eventually, you will fall into a malignant whirlpool of increasing anxiety, helplessness, and depression.

When you make a mistake, and the fault is yours, face up to it. Accept it and take responsibility. But most importantly, develop of correction plan to make sure the mistake is not likely to occur again.

That's what we mean by effective coping—not attacking
and trying to subdue your anxiety or other negative
emotions that result from your mistakes but charting a
new course of action that treats mistakes as providing

*you an opportunity to be less likely to make them in the
future.*

Remember, we're talking behavior patterns here. Defense mechanisms, like rationalism, are chronic, not now-and-then actions. Making excuses is a sign of personality dysfunction, only when you do it all the time.

Imagine a student who received an uncharacteristically low grade on a test. She tells her roommate, "Something's wrong here. I know it's not my fault I got that low grade."

Her roomie says, "Oh, cut the crap and stop rationalizing. You're not perfect, so face up to it and dump the excuses."

The student, however, persists and discovers that the test covered text chapters 6-12, when, in fact, according to the course syllabus, it was supposed to cover chapters 6-10. "I never read chapters 11 and 12 because they weren't supposed to be covered. The prof screwed up big time, and that's why I got the low grade."

The student went to the professor and pointed out the problem, and he adjusted the test scores with questions from chapters 11 and 12 eliminated.

Here's the coping lesson. When you fail, it is totally appropriate to examine why. Carefully and objectively collect evidence to determine if you or someone else is at fault. If it's you, accept it, take responsibility, and take corrective action. If it's someone else, confront them or an appropriate third party to make sure the blame is correctly placed. In this case, you are not being ego-defensive; you are coping well.

WHAT SHOULD BE VERSUS WHAT IS

Do you ever engage in fantasy to comfort yourself? Maybe you have a job interview coming up, or a speech, or a presentation. You're feeling a little stressed, so you let that power of positive thinking kick in: "There's really no need to sweat it. I can handle myself."

Unfortunately, the power of positive thinking is not all it's cracked up to be. It's great to be optimistic about life, but there's a danger if your positive thinking, your optimism, is unrealistic.

A well-known psychologist once told us that growing up, he truly believed he could be a shortstop for the Chicago Cubs. "I played baseball in college, and somewhere along the line, I realized it wasn't going to happen. Contrary to what my folks always told me, I came to the realization that living in America did not mean I could grow up to be anything I wanted to be. No dream was too big, they always said. Well, playing for the Cubbies was too big."

What we see here is the distinction between *what is* and *what should be*. It's nice to dwell on *what should be*, but if you can't translate that thought into realistic action—that is, if you can't turn *what should be* into *what is*—then you must discard *what should be* as unrealistic. Our Cubs wannabe realized that professional baseball was not realistic, so he discarded that fantasy and focused on his academics.

Do you allow your mind to become trapped in the comforting, self-indulgent fantasy of *what should be*? If you do, *what is*, also known as reality, will pass you by, and you will have difficulty coping with all those *what is* things going on in your life.

The power of positive thinking is limited, but the power of positive actions is unlimited.

That's why devising a good coping plan is so important to dealing with your stressors. One of the secrets to effective coping with stress is to engage in positive actions. By positive, we mean actions that bring both you and others satisfaction and comfort. Seeing yourself perform these positive actions will give you a sense of empowerment and will also invest you with optimistic thinking that is based on reality, not on a pipe dream. If you want to be a positive thinker, then engage in positive actions in the here and now.

<>   <>   <>

THINK POSITIVELY! BUT WHAT ELSE?

"You need to keep up a positive attitude if you're going to succeed."

"Use the power of positive thinking when you're faced with difficult challenges."

"If you have a positive outlook on life, you'll be much happier."

"Focus on the positives, and you'll feel much better."

Attitude, positive thinking, optimistic outlook, upbeat focus—you're told that all these positive mindsets will make your life much easier to manage. We don't disagree that a can-do, confident, and proactive viewpoint can help with whatever is facing you and increase your odds of success. But as we said earlier, the power of positive thinking is limited. Our would-be Cub shortstop learned that!

Limited, how? First of all, your optimism must be realistic. You can't surround your attitudes with fantasy, illusions, and imaginary outcomes. You will head quickly toward failure, frustration, disappointment, and self-blame. Second, your positive thoughts and attitudes must be accompanied by actions—your plan. When unaccompanied by concrete, real actions, even positive thoughts vanish in the wind.

When based on positive thinking, actions bring thoughts into reality and allow you to see yourself behaving in productive ways. The best example of this process is when you serve others. Doing so is likely to give you feelings of satisfaction and pleasure, emotions that signal you are coping effectively through personal empowerment, and that you are giving substance to your optimism.

Remember that there is a distinction between "seeking" happiness and "finding" happiness. "Seeking" makes you the think you're the only utensil in the drawer and lulls you into a kind of personal enabling where you see yourself as virtuous and righteous. In a coping context, this orientation is selfish, pompous, smug, and likely to fail.

"Finding," however, allows things like satisfaction and happiness to emerge [see the next section for an explanation of this term] from your altruistic actions and bring you feelings of humility, gratitude, and personal appreciation of your efforts as sincere, open, and authentic. This coping orientation will help you feel you are participating with life in ways that will give you confidence to face your stresses and challenges.

Here's the coping lesson: Don't look for happiness and other wonderful emotions and feelings. Rather, allow yourself to find them by acting in ways that don't make you the center of attention. Depressed, anxious, adrift, lost, unfulfilled, frustrated? Stop constructing a life thinking you are the only architect.

<>   <>   <>

EMERGENCE

Have you ever heard the phrase "The whole is more than the sum of its parts"? The idea is pretty simple: If individual parts are put together in a certain way, something new comes out of the arrangement; something new *emerges*.

Legendary country singer Hank Williams wrote a signature song titled, "I'm So Lonesome I Could Cry." The first line introduces a bird singing and asks, "Did you hear that lonesome whippoorwill?" The remarkable second line states, "He sounds too blue to fly." What an image: Six words describe a bird so down in the dumps that he can't even fly. Now that's sadness!

Let's take those six words in line 2 and mix them up: too, fly, sounds, he, blue, to. Not much emotion or meaning conveyed in that jumble, is there? But when the words are rearranged in a different order, plus put in the context of line 1, something new emerges: a level of sadness that is almost incomprehensible. When the parts are arranged in a given way, something new emerges.

In psychology, the concept of emergence is generally used in the area of perception. But let's see if we can use it more broadly to shed some light on personality functioning and coping with stress. Are you stressed out because you're not happy? Is your life filled with disappointments, anger, anxiety, and feelings of incompetence and low self-esteem? Do you think "I need to be happy"?

Now here's something very important: When you utter this phrase, "I need to be happy," are you thinking you can find happiness just by looking for it? If so, you're making your search all about you. "*I'm* having a hard time!" "*I* deserve better." "*My* needs come first." "*I* need to be happy."

We have two coping problems here: First, effective coping cannot be centered on your needs. Second, happiness is not something you can look for and find. You can't circle a date on your calendar and write, "Today find happiness." It's not something on the ground that you can pick up. Rather, happiness is something that *emerges* from your actions.

Actions are the coping key, but those actions cannot be centered on you. Instead of putting yourself as the most important tool in the toolbox, reduce the part you play. You can accomplish this reduction by allowing your troublesome emotions and interpersonal conflicts to help you increase your sensitivity to others—your empathy toward them—who suffer from conflicts similar to yours. This sensitivity and empathy will encourage you to reach out to help them. The bonus? You will discover ample helpings of personal satisfaction to help you cope better with your own problems. In other words, happiness will emerge from your altruistic—honorable—actions.

Let your values enter your plan. Do other people deserve your attention and help? Is their pain important? If you value them as worthy because they are fellow human beings, you are well on the way to effective coping because you will sense their pain and understand their needs. You will reach out to them, and doing so will bring you the special gift of satisfaction and feeling productive. You will be honorable and a useful part of the human experience.

<> <> <>

HOW MUCH DO YOU PAY YOURSELF?

Kathy Knowles runs a consulting firm dedicated to making businesses more aware of employee needs. Businesses use her services to help increase worker satisfaction, retention, and productivity. She focuses on the general employee factors that are relevant across all types of businesses: pay, opportunity to advance, job meaningfulness, feeling appreciated.

Let's take these items and extrapolate from the workplace to your life. In other words, let's see how you can apply basic human resource principles to helping you design a plan to cope with your life circumstances. To do so, you will need to adjust your thinking a bit and see your life as your workplace and you as both worker and boss.

What do you pay yourself? Are you overly self-critical, always putting yourself down? Give yourself a pay raise—maybe a symbolic pat on the back now and then—by complimenting yourself on a job well done. Watch for the times when you feel pretty good, satisfied, about something you did. Pay attention to when the actions occur and resolve to repeat them when the time is right. Give yourself some positive self-talk: "They said I was really helpful. I need to do stuff like that more often."

Do you give yourself opportunities to grow? If you are going to empower yourself and cope effectively with life, you need to have challenges in front of you and the opportunity to tackle those challenges head on. Doing so will help you develop and improve your skills. Instead of sitting around and stagnating, you must provide yourself with opportunities to venture outside your comfort zone, experience new things, and find ways to improve yourself.

Do your activities provide you with a meaningful life? If a job is not personally meaningful, you are unlikely to enjoy it. And so it is with your life. Your life must be meaningful and give you a sense of purpose if you are to be maximally productive and satisfied with your efforts. This is where your values, morality, integrity, and personal standards—your honor—enter the picture. If you stop looking for some expert to run your life, stop looking for artificial chemical crutches, and stop being passive and dependent, you will cope more effectively and enjoy fulfilling discoveries along a meaningful road of life. You must develop your own moral compass.

Do you appreciate yourself? This item has a lot of overlap with "low pay." How often do you put yourself down and engage in self-criticism? How often do you march in your own special pity parade? How much do you ruminate about the past and how others were always mean and rejecting? Do you complain about how others do not appreciate how hard you try and then internalize that criticism by giving yourself a pessimistic evaluation of your abilities? Obviously, you're not perfect; none of us are. But if you get in a pattern of habitually underappreciating yourself, you will strip yourself of confidence, optimism, and willingness to move forward when confronted with life challenges.

Do you give yourself ownership of your life? This item we add to Knowles's list of how to increase productivity, morale, and satisfaction in employees. Workers should be given the opportunity to participate in the development of company policies; they should be consulted on a regular basis so they feel they are contributing to the decision-making process within the company.

By the same token, you need to develop a sense of ownership about your life. You need to feel confident in assessing what you can and cannot control and, within those boundaries, decide how you should direct your life. When you feel such a sense of ownership, you are less vulnerable to others who would dominate and use you for their purposes; you feel greater autonomy and independence in being able to take charge of your life and move confidently in directions you choose.

<>   <>   <>

FIND YOUR HIDDEN STRENGTHS

We often talk about the importance of doing an honest self-assessment as part of the coping process. Developing a sense of empowerment and facing challenges can be greatly facilitated when you have a good idea of your strengths. Unfortunately, it's easy to overlook them and sell yourself short.

Roxy got married a couple of years out of high school and immediately started having kids. She was strictly a stay-at-home mom. When the youngest child reached her mid-teens, Roxy decided she wanted to get a college degree. The local university had several night-school degree programs, and the one in social work looked good to her.

The road to graduation turned out to be long—seven years—but she did it and was approaching fifty when she graduated. Well before the graduation ceremony, Roxy went to her advisor to get some help with her resume. She lamented, "I've never had any work experience to speak of, and I'm nearly fifty! How can I put a resume together that an employer will notice? I got married thirty years ago right out of high school and have no job experience or skills."

The advisor asked her what she had been doing for the last thirty years. She laughed and said, "I raised four kids and a husband and ran a household."

Over the next ten minutes or so, she and the advisor thought "outside the box" and came up with some "work skills and traits" she had acquired over thirty years of marriage and parenting. What would you include? How about persistent, patient, cook, organizer, planner, psychologist, therapist, listener, problem solver, teacher, first-aid nurse, mediator, mentor, role model, disciplinarian, judge? Are those skills that would transfer to a job?

The point here is pretty basic: When you're faced with challenges, it's easy to sell yourself short and avoid confronting hurdles because you tell yourself, "I don't have the skills to take this on." Until you make an honest and realistic assessment of your skills, however, and allow yourself to think broadly and creatively, you'll never know.

One thing for sure: You don't want to live the rest of your life tormented with thoughts of "I wonder what would have happened if I . . . ?" Go forward, and think creatively about what sorts of skills and abilities you bring to the table!

<> 　 <> 　 <>

DEALING WITH SELF-CRITICISM

Let's say you are doing something that causes you emotional stress. For instance, you feel you're always blaming yourself when things "go south." You're also disgusted with yourself because, deep down, you know it's ridiculous to imagine that you're always to blame when things don't work out.

You get so fed up with all this self-blame that you decide it is time bring this tendency under your control. No one is telling you or forcing you to be self-critical, so you know you can work to control it and do it less often. OK, working from that decision and desire, how do you go about tackling this problem and designing your plan?

First, assess where you are. You need what's called a baseline that tells you how often you criticize yourself each day. To find out, you need to start keeping a record. This is simple enough. Several times during the day, when you have a break from work or home responsibilities, reflect on the past few hours. Note any conversations you have had, and examine your comments and your thoughts for any indications of criticizing yourself. Also write down details of the situation, such as time of day, where the behavior took place, and any other people involved. If you're able, you can also do this recording right after realizing you were just self-critical.

At the end of the day, record the frequency of your self-directed negative comments on a sheet of paper with the date and day of the week. Post this record in a prominent spot where you will easily see it. The number you record will correspond to the more detailed record you kept earlier.

For the first couple of weeks, don't do anything else. Just keep recording those numbers on your posted sheet. There's no need to post the detailed record, but stay organized and keep those records together in a folder.

Don't be surprised if the number of times you engage in self-critical behavior each day begins to drop. This is a nice side effect of the recording procedure. When you record your behavior, you are bringing your actions clearly into your conscious mind, which means you will more likely catch yourself about to take the blame for something and be able to resist doing so.

For instance, you begin to announce to yourself or others, "Well, I guess it's my fault," but you catch it and say to yourself, "Wait a minute, I'm not responsible for this, and I'm not taking the blame." Just becoming aware of your action can help you be your own counselor!

Posting the record can also bring out your competitive juices—that is, as you approach the end of the day, you realize that yesterday you had eight episodes of self-blame, and today you're only up to six. You tell yourself, "If I manage to avoid another episode, I can beat yesterday." If you pull it off, you will give yourself a tremendous reinforcement when you see the chart the next day.

One nasty thing about our undesirable habits is that we don't monitor their occurrence. We usually have no idea how often we do something we would like to stop. Just becoming aware of the action can lower how often it occurs. If that doesn't happen for you, don't sweat it. After a couple of weeks, you will at least know where you are, and you will have that baseline against which to evaluate any steps you take to decrease your habit.

A nice thing about the detailed supplementary notes coordinated to the chart is that you can begin to discern trends. You may notice that your self-blame is more frequent in the presence of certain other people, or in specific situations such as in a meeting, or when you're tired. Keeping the record makes you aware of your actions and can help you get a handle on specific events, places, and people that are strongly associated with when the actions take place.

A major part of being able to change your undesirable behavior is becoming aware of when and where the unwanted actions occur.

Once you're aware of those situations, you can reduce your exposure to them, plus be more on guard when you're in those situations. Again, awareness is the key. Most of our bad habits take hold of us because we're totally unaware of when and where we're exercising them. Find those situations that bring on self-critical comments, and then you can take corrective action aimed at appropriate targets.

The next steps are up to you. Find techniques to reduce your self-blame tendencies that work for you. Remember that one size does not fit all. What worked for your neighbor or friend will not necessarily work for you. And keep up the chart because you will be able to evaluate precisely the effectiveness of any technique you try.

Above all, remember that you are changing your lifestyle. You're not in this for a week or a month. You are literally modifying how you act in specific situations. It takes time, practice, perseverance, and patience. There is only one way to win this fight—that is, to treat it like warfare. You are the general in charge of your thoughts and actions, and failure is simply not an option. Will you win every battle? Of course not. You will always have slips and setbacks. Ultimately, however, they must not deter you from feeling that you are winning the war.

A LESSON FROM A PRESIDENT

In 1963, VP Lyndon Johnson assumed the presidency when John Kennedy was assassinated. In the election of 1964, Johnson was elected president on his own merits. In *Leadership in Turbulent Times*, historian Doris Kearns Goodwin describes how Johnson enjoyed success in his domestic goals, notable civil rights, but failed miserably when confronted with the Vietnam War. If we analyze his actions in these areas in the context of the coping model we present in this book—*acceptance, accountability, humility, empathy,* and development of a *coping plan*—the outcomes are understandable.

On the home front, Johnson accepted the realities of congressional power. He had served a total of twenty-four years in Congress, twelve in the House and twelve in the Senate, and he knew the dynamics as well as anyone. This knowledge allowed him to appreciate what he could and could not expect to control, and he was willing to be accountable for overcoming the obstacles. He knew how to shape legislative plans that included an empathetic and humble appreciation of others' opinions. He knew how to engage in honest communication with adversaries and knew the importance of compromise. A profoundly religious man, he knew how to play the "spiritual card" with calls for social justice, again showing his empathy.

Vietnam, however, was quite another matter. He was not able to accept the futility of American military involvement. He was out of his element in this arena, and year after year, it seemed that planning for "victory" was haphazard, almost random. As failures mounted, he turned away from personal accountability to "experts" for advice on how to stave off catastrophe; he became dependent on their point of view, a situation that, as we have seen, blocks effective coping.

Johnson's approach to Vietnam also involved neither humility nor empathy. Instead, his actions were designed to avoid defeat, and we have said repeatedly that avoidance of challenges is completely incompatible with effective coping. Eventually, he began looking for scapegoats to blame for the disaster unfolding around him. The realities continued to weigh him down, however, and he took the one avoidance action remaining: He announced he would not run for reelection in 1968.

Our analysis of Johnson's domestic success and foreign failure shows that the coping principles we have been describing are not limited to everyday conflicts and challenges. Indeed, our coping model is relevant for national leaders trying to navigate the challenges of presidential leadership. Thus, it is appropriate to ask, "How are you approaching the stress in your life? Are you the Civil Rights Johnson or the Vietnam Johnson?"

RELIGION, SPIRITUALITY, AND COPING

If you have a set of personal values, standards, a social conscience, and a moral compass grounded in a strong, sincere, intrinsic faith system, you have a leg up on coping. While not necessary for effective coping, such a spirituality definitely helps things along.

Interestingly, those who regularly attend church services, pray, and read scripture are more likely to have low blood pressure and stronger immune systems. They are less likely to suffer depression from stressful life events. When they do get depressed, they are more likely to recover. They have a lower incidence of cardiovascular disease and cancer and are likely to live longer.

Before you decide to run out and praise the Lord, however, be aware that religious people have these health benefits because their faith system—their spirituality—is part of their overall approach to life. Sincerely and intrinsically spiritual—we will use "spiritual" instead of "religious" to make the point that our comments are not limited to those connected to a formal church setting or to any particular religion—people tend to have positive thinking styles about life. Events in their lives are not perceived as random and accidental but are seen as part of an overall pattern. Furthermore, bad things are seen more as challenges to be dealt with, not as something beyond their control and potentially devastating.

Sincerely and intrinsically spiritual people tend to give meaning to both good and bad events in their lives. They see an overall pattern that suggests a purpose to life. This outlook gives them a protective sense of coherence to life. It is also important to note that this sense of coherence increases the likelihood that they will take care of their bodies, reach out to serve others, and nurture their relationships with valued family and friends. In short, their sincere and intrinsic spirituality both allows and encourages them to participate in the grandeur of life.

As we noted earlier, there's no secret to maximizing the probability of being physically and emotionally healthy and feeling good. These states emerge from those things under your control: the behaviors you engage in and the thoughts you maintain each day—in short, the perceptions and interpretations you make about events and people around you. A sense of coherence and purpose to life, and the confidence to meet the challenges of life, evolve from these lifestyles. These are the attributes that give you honor.

Honor carries with it what we might call *intrinsic sincerity*. That means your internal compass, no matter where it comes from, is genuine, sincere. For instance, merely paying lip service to religious commitment just won't cut it. If you go to church, or expound to others about your faith just so they will think more highly of you, that's an insincerity that brings dishonor. That use of religion to obtain non-spiritual goals will not translate into better physical and psychological health.

For a personal faith system to foster the honorable self and be part of a healthy and productive lifestyle, that faith must be intrinsic and part of a greater spirituality; it must be valued for itself, not for the material rewards, status, or power it may bring. Faith that brings good health and a feeling that you can exercise some control and direction in your life is a faith that is genuine. Such faith can be a principal motivating force in your life and something that influences your everyday behavior and decisions.

CHAPTER 7

RELAXATION EXERCISES

PREPARE YOURSELF MENTALLY

You may be one of the many people who suffers anxiety that causes you significant stress in specific situations. Remember, however, that before you confront the difficulty, there are several preliminary steps to take to help you.

First of all, ask yourself, *"Is this a situation I can control?"* There are only two things you can directly control: *your* thoughts and *your* actions. If your problem involves the thoughts and actions of others, then your answer to the question must be "no," and you should move on to other issues in your life.

If your answer is "yes," then ask yourself, *"What specific features of the situation make me anxious and want to avoid it?"* List the troublesome aspects of the situation and when they occur. Then you can move on to taking action to cope with the situation.

If you know the event is coming, expect to be anxious. *Do not deny the inevitable and tell yourself, "I'll be fine."* You won't be fine, and the anxiety will overwhelm you.

Remember that your emotions are part of you, so *don't apologize to yourself, criticize yourself, or feel ashamed.* When you identify, evaluate, and analyze the events that bring on the anxiety, you will be better able to accept your anxiety and confront those events.

Don't focus on the stress and anxiety you feel. Instead, focus on the actions you can take to deal with your problem. For example, "I do not enjoy my job, but I refuse to answer ads for other jobs because I'm afraid I will fail in the interview." Now you have something specific to attack—not the stress itself, but your fear of failure in an interview. The different focus will help you modify your thinking and think of the event as a challenge that will give you an opportunity to show your skills, as long as you prepare. In other words, *you* are accountable.

Be realistic about stress. *Are you ruled by irrational thoughts*, such as, "I must be perfect and succeed in everything I do or I am a worthless person"? A more realistic thought would be, "If I fail, I will examine what I did wrong and take steps to correct my mistake so I will be less likely to fail the next interview." If you're stressed about driving to a meeting across town, how difficult can it be to say, "I have no control over how bad the traffic will be, but I can leave early so heavy traffic will not make me late. I can also use my relaxation methods (see below) if I feel stressed, and I can map out alternative routes in advance in case traffic backs up."

Let's face it. Those who have trouble coping with stress spend too much time focusing on their emotions. "I'm so stressed out—anxious and frightened—I'm going to lose control!" Well, take a deep breath and focus on the realities: Having emotions that cause you stress is a normal, unavoidable aspect of life, and feeling stressed does not make you inferior to others. You can schedule stressful events under your control when you expect relatively few demands and change in other areas of your life. You can reserve some time for yourself each day to relax—if only for a few minutes—and take a walk, listen to music, or trade jokes with a friend. You can commit to and nurture important aspects of your life, such as marriage, career, children, friendships and family. You can stay away from self-defeating actions, like excessive eating, drinking, spending, or gambling. These are avoidance actions and will only lead to increased stress.

When faced with stress, your best bet is to recognize it, accept it as real, and attack it.

Stress is not the issue; what you do about
the stress is the issue.

Accept the fact that life is supposed to have some stress. Marriage, Christmas, having a baby, retirement, seeking a job promotion—all are stressful and require adjustment. Should you avoid them? Should you tolerate a mediocre job to avoid the stress of seeking a new and more challenging position? Should you avoid commitment in a relationship because you fear the stress of marriage? Should you avoid ending an abusive relationship because you fear the stress of "making it on your own"? "Are people who resist change and avoid stress better off in the long run?"

If you answer "yes" to these questions, you are avoiding life, not living it. Avoidance is a form of denial that says, "I'm going to ignore you, so please go away." But it won't go away; denial and avoidance will not make stress magically disappear. Your best bet is to accept your emotional reaction as a part of your reality, and resolve to confront it and use it to your advantage. That is the honorable thing to do!

The steps we have listed can help you organize your thinking about anxiety issues and help you see the best ways, in general, to carry out actions to confront those issues. Before doing so, however, it helps to be able to calm down and relax a bit. Your thinking will be clearer and more rational if you can compose yourself and soothe your body.

Let's look at some relaxation and focus techniques that you can use to prepare yourself to be able to focus on some of the actions we suggested above. The remainder of the material in this section is provided by Brian Cook, licensed counselor and director of the Counseling Center at King's College. We thank him for sharing relaxation methods that he uses in his practice. We also included this material in our earlier book, *Using Psychology to Cope with Everyday Stress.*

<>   <>   <>

A USEFUL MENTAL IMAGE

Coping with stress is like walking across a room while carrying a cup of coffee or a glass of iced tea. If you think about it and break it down, there are several parts in that process that make the trip across the room successful. The same is true for coping.

You have to be *aware* of your situation. In carrying the cup or glass, your pace and speed will matter, any obstacles on the floor will influence how you proceed, and how you set the cup down will determine the success of the trip.

You may have to *make adjustments* concerning the contents of the cup or glass as you proceed—that is, if the liquid tips to one side of the container, there's a risk some may spill out. In this case, you will have to adjust your wrist and level the container to prevent the spillage. You might have to do this balancing act several times over the course of the trip. In fact, you might even have to stop to let the liquid settle back into place before you take your next step.

In addition to a stationary object in your path, you might have to change your course because a new obstacle appears, like the dog or cat suddenly blocking your path. You must always be prepared for the unexpected.

When you get across the room and finally set down the cup or glass, it's important to evaluate how you did. *Reflect* on the trip, and decide if there is anything that needs to be "cleaned up." If so, it's best to address it right then.

I hope you can see that by following this imagery, coping is really one big balancing act in your life. Living is represented by carrying the cup or glass across the room; the contents of your life are constantly changing. Coping is dealing with those changes in the contents—finding the actions that work best for you.

What follows are some of the techniques I use with clients to help them relax and deal better with troublesome situations, especially those that arouse anxiety. Whenever you face one of those situations, before trying one of these techniques, you might want to picture yourself carrying a container of liquid across a room. Doing so can help you focus on a task at hand and not on the emotion you are feeling.

A BREATHING TECHNIQUE

One of the most fundamental problems with anxiety and stress is that we tend to project into the future—that is, we tell ourselves, "I'm going to be so tense next week when I take that driving test. I'll probably lose my concentration and fail." No doubt you have been guilty of this sort of "future thinking." How does it make you feel? Do you agree that such anticipation only stirs up your emotions and raises your inner tension? Is this how you want to spend the next week, mired in some sort of dread condition?

How about learning to refocus your thinking back to the present to reduce this inner tension and to take charge of your current reality? How about living in the present moment to prepare yourself for the future? The techniques below have been shown to be quite effective in helping this process by helping you relax and block out distracting thoughts.

Do some deep breathing. When you're anxious, one of the first things to change is your breathing rate. How can you get your normal respiration back? First, empty your lungs; "blow out the birthday candles," so to speak. Exhale all the air you can. Then take a deep breath in through your nose for about five seconds. Repeat five to ten times, but don't focus on the number.

Next, try to gain a rhythm, such as three seconds in through the nose and three seconds out through the mouth. No need to focus on timing things; just make each phase last a moderate period. With practice several times each day, you will become quite proficient at loosening yourself up in a stressful situation.

USING YOUR SENSES

Along with the breathing technique, you can use your senses and the 5-4-3-2-1 progression. This method uses your five senses to orient your thinking to the present. First, picture five things you can see around you and describe each using an adjective or two. Ideally, find objects that give you a relaxed feeling. For instance, "I see a black chair. I see a table that has a computer monitor on it. The table is on a blue rug. I see a window and bright sunshine outside. Near the window is a tree full of green leaves."

Next, describe four things you can touch, again using an adjective or two. "A part of my chair has a metal frame that is cool to the touch." Next, describe three things you can hear—"There is a soft hum of the air conditioner." Then two things you can smell—it's OK to lean over and smell the flowers on the desk. Finally, one thing you can taste— take a swig of your water or coffee. You can do these in any order, but typically, it works best if you follow this order of the senses as it is hard to engage a number of things for each sense. For example, it's hard to smell five things at once.

SERIAL SEVENS

Another distraction technique is called serial 7s. Say the sentence "I will be a more positive person" seven times. Then go back and say each word of the sentence seven times: "I, I, I, I, I, I, I, will, will, will, will, will, will, will," etc. Then go back and say the entire sentence seven more times. You should pace yourself and follow this procedure about one word per second, fast enough so other thoughts can't come through and distract you. This is a good technique to get your mind off whatever started making you anxious. Once again, it is best to combine this method with your breathing exercise. Also, don't worry about the exact count. The point here is to distract you, redirect your thinking, not make sure you can count to seven!

DETAILED FOCUSING

A distraction technique that works for many people involves focusing on one thing in great detail. When you start to feel anxious, this technique has you focus on one thing, imagining every possible detail. Then take each detail, name it, and focus on various characteristics. If you picture a car, for instance, how many details about a car can you name? There's the engine, door handles, hood, trunk, steering wheel, etc. This sort of mental effort can go a long way toward getting your mind off the topic that was making you anxious and serve to relax a lot of inner tension. If you still feel anxious after you try this once, move on to another object and continue to count the details. As always, pair this process with your breathing exercise.

PERSONAL PLEASURES

Like everyone else, you have many small things that you find personally satisfying and relaxing. It could be an object, a mental image, an activity, just about anything. It is these small things that often have the most effect in helping you cope with stress and anxiety; perhaps a music playlist of your favorite songs, going for a short walk, playing with the family pet, stretching to increase your blood flow and oxygen flow. Identify those things, and if possible, activate one of them when you feel stressed. At the very least, think about how you will use one of those things later when appropriate.

To give yourself some reassurance, write on index cards those personal things that bring you tranquility and serenity. Keep the cards handy so you know you will have a quick and easy way to reduce any stress that may be coming and readily have activities you can do that work to calm you and bring you some peace of mind.

DAILY THOUGHT REVIEW

Finally, it's useful to "check in"—not obsess about!—with yourself throughout the day. What have you been thinking about? Have your thoughts been realistic, rational, and positive? Have you been excessively focusing on some problem that may not be real or may not be under your control? The check-in process allows you to evaluate your mental status during a typical day, failing to do so can get you into all sorts of problems, and before you know it, you have thought yourself into emotional turmoil.

CHAPTER 8

A WORD ABOUT DEPRESSION

I'm under so much stress, I feel like I'm losing it. The boss sends me out on two- or three-night trips about once a month. I feel so guilty about leaving my wife with three teenage daughters—thirteen, fifteen, seventeen. You want stress? Live with three teenage girls. My wife is patient and understanding, but I know she resents me having to go away, and she wishes I had another job. Sometimes I feel so much stress, anxiety, guilt—you name it. I just want to crawl in a hole. I feel I'm suffering from depression and need to get some meds from the doctor. Other times I wonder if I'm truly mentally ill.

This guy's commentary is really not all that unusual. Sometimes normal stress burdens seem to get so out of hand that worries about being "crazy" or suffering from a severe mental illness, depression, just add to the overall stress level. Let's devote some discussion of these terms within the limits of the stressors we have been talking about in this book. First, a brief look at "mental illness" and then a review of depression.

DO COPING PROBLEMS MEAN I AM MENTALLY ILL?

Short answer: No.

Most people think of "mental illness" as analogous to "physical illness." They see "illness" as a black/white affair, which might work when talking about physical illness: You're either sick or you're well. You have a fever or don't. You have appendicitis or don't. You have cancer, kidney stones, a broken leg, or you don't.

When it comes to "mental illness" things are more subtle. There usually is no clear line separating being ill and being healthy when it comes to our psychological functioning. In fact, unless you have a clear organic—that is, physical—condition (such as brain damage), you should avoid the phrase "mental illness."

Unfortunately, the term "mental illness" is being tossed around a lot these days because of "unexpected" behavior, be it inexplicable mass shootings or unusual actions at high levels of government. People using the phrase, however, really don't understand the consequences of applying this description to someone.

"Mental illness" is a negative label we apply to someone who is behaving "strangely" or in ways that bother us. The label carries all kinds of negative stereotypes, biases, and evaluations against the person so labeled. Unfortunately, like any label, it tends to stick and guide our behavior toward that person, even in the face of contradictory evidence. Rosenhan's classic study in 1973 illustrated the effect quite nicely.

In a now-classic research investigation done in the early 1970s, Rosenhan and some of his graduate students got themselves admitted to various mental hospitals by going to admissions offices and complaining about hearing voices. All were successfully admitted and diagnosed with psychotic disorders. Once admitted, they acted entirely normal, but were never discovered. Their treatment consisted mostly of pills to take, which they managed to flush down the toilet. After an average stay of three weeks, all were released with a diagnosis of "schizophrenia in remission."

One of the lessons of the study was how the fake patients were treated by the professional staff as real patients. Even though the students behaved normally, once they were labeled "mentally ill," everything they said and did was evaluated in that context. One student took lots of notes, behavior that was recorded as "compulsive note-taking." Had he been labeled as a student, his note-taking would have been seen as quite normal.

I [CB] remember an episode that took place in the early 1970s. I was supervising an internship for a student whose placement was in a local psychiatric institution. When I first made an on-site visitation, I reported to the main office, gave my name and position, and the name of the student I was supervising. Once all the formalities were done, the receptionist pointed to an employee standing nearby and said he would escort me to the student's placement area.

Along the way, the employee answered a variety of questions I had about the facility, plus made a number of detours so he could give me somewhat of an informal tour of various areas. When we finally reached the department where my student was working that day, I thanked my guide, and he went on his way. Imagine my surprise when my student identified my escort as a patient in the facility. Obviously, the patient was high-functioning and stabilized on medication, which really was the case with most of the patients, but I was still quite surprised.

The point of this story is simple: In my mind, I had initially identified my guide as an employee, so I never thought twice about second-guessing any of his behavior. On the other hand, had the receptionist said to me, "That gentleman is one of our patients, and he will escort you to where you student is working today," I bet I would have felt a little uncomfortable and certainly not asked many questions about the facility. I would have been eager to reach our destination and send him on his way.

Imagine if you walked into a meeting at work and spotted someone unfamiliar. You ask a colleague, "Who's that guy over there? I've never seen him before."

"Oh, that's Ron," your friend says. "Seems he's been in a psychiatric institution for several months and just got out. Apparently, the boss knows him and decided to give him a job."

How will you look at Ron? Will you rush over and welcome him to the organization? Will you watch his every movement for signs of pathology? Will that label "mentally ill" that is attached to him influence your interpretation of his actions? If Ron swats his hand at a mosquito you don't see, will you think, "Omigod, he's hallucinating!" If your colleague does the same thing, of course, you will probably conclude, "Must be a mosquito in here."

The message we want to convey is that the term "mental illness" is a label that observers put on someone whose behavior is atypical, it is also a label that carries all sorts of negative stereotypes, and finally, applying the label leads to erroneous perceptions of actions we observe in another. The bottom line is that using the phrase is probably not at all helpful in our everyday interactions, so don't obsess about whether or not your coping outcomes mean you are mentally ill.

<>   <>   <>

GENERAL MISCONCEPTIONS ABOUT DEPRESSION

If you're like most people, when you think of the word "depression," your thinking is clouded by a lot of misconceptions. For instance, depression is not the same as unhappiness. You have bad days and get down in the dumps. Who doesn't? This *situational sadness*, however, will lift with a change in the situation or in your perception of the situation. Feeling unhappy and dissatisfied at times is not really depression.

Here are four additional complications that can make evaluation of genuine depression difficult:

First, disengaging from life—what we call *subtle suicide* in our book of the same title—can be confused with depression. In a formal diagnostic context, subtle suicide—characterized by ambivalence, apathy, and a "Who cares?" attitude toward life—can be distinguished from chronic depressive disorder. Unfortunately, many people who show this ambivalence toward life are often misdiagnosed as depressed and prescribed antidepressant medication, which doesn't work in this case.

Second, in the medical profession, most diagnoses of depression are not made on the basis of formal psychological assessment. Informal diagnoses can lead to diagnostic errors and result in inappropriate treatments. For instance, anxiety, anger, and other emotions brought about by life circumstances can be confused with depression.

Third, in those cases where clinical depression is present, it can be accompanied by other psychological dysfunctions. Focusing only on depression, whether through medication or counseling, will not work if the other conditions are ignored.

Fourth, much research shows that psychiatric medications are no better than a placebo for low and moderate levels of depression. Also, remember that there are no medications that will empower you or that will develop an action plan for you to navigate the challenges of life and develop more satisfying and productive actions.

The bottom line of this confusing state of affairs is be cautious and seek information from a variety of sources.

If you feel you have a persistent, chronic problem with your mood that significantly interrupts your daily activities, you should consult both a psychiatrist and a psychologist.

This combination will provide you with a thorough psychological evaluation and diagnosis, decrease the risk of diagnostic errors, and help you work actively as a participant in developing a treatment plan that may include medications.

PERSISTENT DEPRESSIVE DISORDER

You have probably heard of bipolar disorder and major depression but perhaps not persistent depressive disorder (PDD). The symptoms of PDD tend to be subtle compared with bipolar and major depression, conditions with more severe and dramatic symptoms. For instance, suicide attempts, psychiatric hospitalization, and the need for antidepressant medication are much more common with major depression and bipolar disorder.

PDD is largely a cognitive condition, a way of perceiving and thinking about events in your life in a negative way. In that sense, PDD is a type of depression that fits somewhat, not perfectly, into the coping themes of this book: acceptance, accountability, humility, empathy, and planning.

If you think negative thoughts about yourself, you are going to feel pretty rotten, you are likely to avoid coping challenges, and you are more likely to get depressed. Imagine waking up feeling pretty good but going through the day repeatedly telling yourself, "I'm incompetent. I'm going to fail. I can't do anything worthwhile. I'm a disappointment to others. I'm such a klutz, everyone feels sorry for me." How do you think you will feel at the end of the day? Pretty good or down in the dumps?

If you feel you might suffer from depression but tend to write it off as just having some temporary problems dealing with life, you could be one of the "silent sufferers" afflicted with PDD. You go to work or school, you care for your loved ones, and you generally function in the normal range of activities. But you have this gnawing feeling that most people seem to enjoy life more than you do.

You feel you have more than your share of pessimism, guilt, lack of interest, appetite fluctuations, low self-esteem, chronic fatigue, social withdrawal, and concentration difficulties. You have a chronic discontent with yourself, and your negative thinking has become a way of life.

The seeds of PDD are usually planted in childhood or adolescence and result from poor development and guidance in developing social skills, optimistic thinking, and a belief that you can deal with challenges. Early in life, you accept that you are helpless and dwell on the negative, and you experience a steady buildup of stress.

You might seek psychological help. If you are diagnosed with "depression," you will likely get a prescription for antidepressant medication. Unfortunately, medication can be effective with major depression and bipolar disorder but is usually ineffective for PDD. About the best that can be expected is a temporary "kick-start" to developing new thinking and actions *with the help of psychological counseling.*

PDD is primarily an avoidance issue, the sorts of things that we discuss in this book. You develop long-standing actions that allow you to avoid facing challenges and maintain your symptoms. You probably tend to avoid facing and dealing with stressors—unfortunately, the very stressors that cause and sustain your depression. In other words, like many of the stories we describe in this book, you avoid the very stressors that you need to confront.

Your depression is accompanied by actions that rob you of energy, motivation, and positive attitudes that are needed to break free of your avoidance patterns. As a result, your depression probably creates problems in other areas, such as social interactions, concentration and focus, alcohol/drug issues, etc. You must not despair though. Burdened with PDD, you can still learn to challenge and face your demons by following the lessons throughout this book, engaging in professional counseling, and probably without long-term medication use.

<> <> <>

SEASONAL AFFECTIVE DEPRESSION

Let's take a look at a particular type of depression that occurs primarily during the winter months. This condition raises a lot of issues that can be approached in the context of the coping model we develop in this book.

Every September Lynn gives her psychiatrist's office a call and asks for a renewal of her antidepressant medication. She tells them she's feeling fine and hasn't taken any meds since last April. But winter is coming, and she knows that come late October, she will begin to feel "down" as those winter blues set in. She wants to get a running start and start the meds so they will have already "kicked in" by November, and she will cut off the depression at the pass, so to speak. Her strategy is like getting a flu shot before the flu season sets in.

Lynn suffers from SAD, an acronym for seasonal affective depression, also called seasonal affective disorder or seasonal adjustment disorder. This depression hits people in the winter—some think as a result of reduced sunlight. To combat her depression, Lynn has chosen psychiatric medication. If that plan works for her, so be it. It's hard to argue with success. For those who would like to forgo medication, however, there are alternatives to dealing with SAD.

As we noted above, some professionals say SAD results from reduced sunlight, which causes biochemical imbalances in the brain. Thus, you can treat SAD with exposure to artificial light during the winter by sitting in front of a special lamp for an hour or so each day before sunrise and again after sunset. The idea is to extend the amount of time your brain is bathed in light each day and, thus, maintain an appropriate biochemical balance that results in a good mood. These special lamps, by the way, can be purchased for several hundred dollars. Obtaining a good "brain tan" is not cheap!

Still another approach to SAD is in line with themes we try to develop in this book. This approach emphasizes personal empowerment, autonomous action, and taking control of your behavior during the winter months. If such a "treatment" brings relief, some feel it is preferable to depending on a drug.

Before considering this non-drug option, however, let's note some of the stressors that the winter months bring. SAD comes along when the weather is reminding you of the long winter months ahead, at least for some parts of the country. These months can be a tough time for those who live in the northern sections of the country because they're cooped up in the house for several months. It gets dark earlier, and it's harder to take those enjoyable strolls around the neighborhood after dinner. So you decide you might as well stay in the house, a decision that causes you to gain weight, which further depresses you when you look at the scale in January.

You're also more likely to get sick during the winter months. The flu season kicks in around late October/early November, just when daylight saving time ends. You hate the darkness that comes earlier each evening. In northern locales, you also worry about road conditions when there's ice and snow. And how about all those weather school delays and cancelations that lead to anxiety about what to do with the kids? More winter stress!

Some researchers say the increased darkness may have an adverse effect on the immune system. A weakened immune system during the winter could explain why you seem to get sick more often and why flu season corresponds with the cold, dark winter months. So on top of all those other winter stressors, you worry about getting sick. And if you do get sick, you're more likely to feel depressed. It's a "perfect storm"!

In the middle of it all is the dreaded Christmas season! Presents to buy and wrap, homes to decorate, relatives who visit, travel plans if you visit them instead, parties to attend, secret Santa responsibilities at work, excessive booze and food, hosting social events, and on and on as the stress continues to build. Who wouldn't be depressed?

Maybe SAD need not be such a big deal, at least if you approach winter the right way. First of all, it would help if you used some coping techniques to reduce some of the anxiety you're feeling. Here's a Christmas example offered by Dr. Carlea Dries:

> "A couple of weeks after Halloween I noticed my neighbor's house was already fully decked out for Christmas. I almost let myself suffer some anxiety about being decoratively-challenged and embarrassingly late for Christmas, but I caught myself. 'Wait a minute. Just because neighbor is 6 weeks ahead of the curve, I don't have to be; my house can wait a few weeks for the decorations.'
>
> Dries continues, "But I couldn't stop my brain from kicking into overdrive trying to determine how many days before the holiday invitations come in and the holiday cards go out; how many gifts do I need to pick out, wrap, and deliver; how many cookies do I have to bake and refrain from eating; how many surprise

guests will appear with tidings of good cheer; how many deadlines do I have to meet during this most wonderful time of the year; how many bills will I be able to pay; how many times will I have to clean the house . . . Well, you get the idea. I was suddenly flooded with stress."

Dries adds, "Then I allowed myself the opportunity to stop, breathe, and refocus. I could try to positively reframe those palpitation-inducing thoughts, such as how lucky I am to have such good relationships in my life that hordes of people will come visit. But I can remember the power of the word 'No.' Just because I receive an invitation to an event doesn't mean I have to attend; just because I've always given presents to the child-age cousins in the family doesn't mean I have to this year. Saying 'No' frees me up to be the better version of myself during the occasions when I say, 'Yes.' I won't be as tired, cranky, or Scrooge-like. Instead I will be able to fully focus on the things that matter—special time with those I hold dear."

Great advice! Take control. Of course, one thing we can't control is winter weather. How do we deal with that? First of all, let's ask if there is even a relationship between our moods and the weather. We'll give that question a definite "yes." Researchers at the Virginia Institute for Psychiatric and Behavioral Genetics found that mood and thinking ability both increased with warmer, pleasant temperatures and sunny, pleasant weather.

But it's not that simple. The researchers also found that when assigned to work on tasks outside on warm, sunny days, the mood of the research participants definitely increased; for those assigned to complete the tasks inside, however, even when pleasant weather conditions prevailed outside, mood was lower. So the positive effect of weather depended on *where the person was working* during those nice weather conditions. Working outside was definitely better than working inside. Isn't this exactly what happens every spring? Warm April days come after weeks of cold weather that has driven you inside. And now, almost overnight, there is opportunity for outdoor activities. So you get outside and do more and you feel great!

There's a key word here: *activity*. Is it possible that you might develop mood swings in the winter months because you *change your routine* and give in to the darkness? All those worries about the dangers imposed by night driving, bad-weather driving, flying home for the holidays, becoming snowbound in an airport, getting the flu, or a host of other self-imposed concerns—all resulting from a negative psychological response to the winter season—just tie you up in knots. So you curl up on the couch and give up. You're less likely to go out to dinner and parties, host social events at home, or engage in outdoor hobbies and recreation.

Here's our non-pharmaceutical take on SAD: The key to maintaining a good mood during the dark months is to maintain a steady "diet" of activity, just like during the summer months. You should schedule special events and activities that you'll look forward to and enjoy. Release your empathy and seek out service activities. There are numerous opportunities for helping others during the winter, especially during the holiday season. Remember, the winter months bring special challenges to many people, so put your honorable self into gear: reach out to others, get involved in charity projects, volunteer at a homeless shelter during the coldest time of the year. Get out there and be with people.

How about your outdoor activities during the winter? Obviously, some are gone, like the softball team, but you don't have to give up walking. Sure, you have to bundle up in January to take that walk, but doing so is better than sitting on your butt.

We know a serious outside walker who is also a serious winter hater! Still, she never lets the winter weather defeat her when it comes to walking outside. During the winter, she bundles up in layers of sweat clothes, scarves, and windbreakers. Then armed with her music device and earphones, out she goes. Her only concession to winter weather is the route she takes. If there is snow on the ground, many of her summer walking paths are just not accessible, so she changes the route accordingly. She always returns home about an hour later, moaning and groaning about the evils of winter. But she is invigorated and feels good physically and mentally after these winter walks.

We think the fundamental idea behind SAD is flawed. As winter approaches and the days get shorter, if you want to believe that you are doomed to get depressed because of reduced sunlight, that's your choice. But remember, *darkness is not going to make you depressed; it's what you do during the darkness that makes the difference.*

The winter months should be viewed as a challenging time to continue with those activities that give you pleasure and a sense of control in your life, not as a time to hibernate! What you do is under your control; the weather is not!

Would it surprise you to hear someone say, "When I go outside in winter, I find myself invigorated. It really *is* invigorating to take a walk in the dark when it's cold and the snow crunches. It also makes me feel like a warrior woman when I do something like that. Frostbite warnings are no match for me!" Anyone who thinks about winter in this way is coping quite well.

We couldn't say it better. If you have a tendency to get down in the dumps during those long winter months and want to purchase one of the expensive lamps to bathe your brain in artificial sunlight, that's up to you. If you want to start taking antidepressant medication in September, well, that's your choice too. We think, however, you will be much better "inoculated" and feel more empowered against winter's psychological dangers if you continue your regular exercise and other activity routines during the winter, plus be willing to take on new things.

Activity is the antidote to depression.

Spit in winter's face! Before you know it, you'll be venturing outside to be bathed in that warm April sunshine!

<>   <>   <>

A PLAN FOR *MODERATE* DEPRESSION

This section—in fact, this entire book—is not intended for anyone suffering from major Depression, a disorder that causes a persistent feeling of sadness and loss of interest, and can profoundly affect your normal day-to-day activities. You may even feel at times as if life isn't worth living. Major depression is not about having the "blues" that you can snap out of when some of your life circumstances change; it is a level of depression that may require long-term treatment, including both medication and psychotherapy.

Major depression symptoms can include feelings of emptiness, hopelessness, worthlessness, and guilt; lack of energy; disturbances in appetite; angry outbursts over small matters; thoughts of death and suicide attempts; sleep disturbances; loss of interest in activities that used to bring you pleasure; difficulty thinking and concentrating.

If you show most of these symptoms on a regular basis, you should seek professional help from a psychiatrist or psychologist. You will likely profit from antidepressant medication and even require short-term hospitalization. Don't take any chances.

With those cautions in mind, let's summarize—within the limits of what we discuss in this book—some specific actions you can take to confront *moderate levels of depression*, such as PDD. Please remember, however, that effective coping requires honest self-discovery and awareness of your strengths and weaknesses. Unfortunately, if you don't work at translating your traits, even your weaknesses, into productive actions, you will have no anchor to reality. This process is crucial in confronting moderate levels of depression: If you cannot "translate yourself" into concrete actions, you will feel you have nowhere to go and likely will remain depressed.

Ask yourself,

> "Am I truly depressed or just unhappy?"
> "Are my problems related to anger or anxiety that make me look and feel depressed?"

"Do I have experiences like childhood abuse or neglect that I have never faced?"

Monitor your daily behavior to look for *avoidance* actions you may be taking to reduce stress in life.

It's natural to feel unhappiness, anxiety, anger, and other emotions brought about by current life circumstances. When it happens, don't tell yourself "I'm depressed" and crawl under a rock. Tell yourself, "I have to identify and deal with the situations that bring me down."

Be vigilant about your health. Exercise, diet, frequent medical checkups, an optimistic attitude—these are just a sample of things you can do to take better control of your life and feel more empowered.

As much as possible, continue your normal exercise routines during the winter.

Identify actions that bring you confidence, assertiveness, enjoyment, and satisfaction. List situations in which you can express those actions and put yourself in those situations as much as possible. These actions help inoculate you against feeling "depressed."

At the end of the day, write down your activities and how they made you feel. Use that information to your advantage tomorrow.

Get involved in charity projects. Reach out and serve others.

Be cautious with psychiatric medications. They are generally no better than a placebo for low and moderate levels of depression. Plus, there is no medication that will provide you with a coping plan.

POSTSCRIPT

When you cope with the stresses of everyday living, you have chosen to live. Coping with life is the opposite of avoiding life. It is unfortunate that too often too many people choose not to face their problems—to stay in their comfort zone—and let life pass them by. Their choice, of course, gives them an easy road to travel in the short run, but over the long haul, they constantly fight the gnawing reality festering inside them that "I could do better."

Facing up to stress—accepting it, confronting it, attacking it—puts you on a rocky road that forces you to carry a stress load that cries out, "I can't handle this!" But you can, and that's why you persist. You discover that the obstacles in your life road are not obstacles—they are the road. Choosing to travel this road brings you long-term benefits: empowerment, self-esteem, a healthy connection to yourself and others—you come closer to a humble realization of your potential, as who you are emerges from empathetic actions in service of others. You discover your honorable self and the humanity that comprises it: your integrity, ethics, decency, morality, and conscience.

Lightning Source UK Ltd.
Milton Keynes UK
UKHW041913031120
372650UK00011BB/1039/J